Wines from Chile

Wines from Chile

Jürgen Mathäss

QUÉ MÁS

© 1997 Qué Más, Amsterdam & Cologne

ISBN 90 5496 036 1

Qué Más is an imprint of The Pepin Press BV
POB 10349
1001 EH Amsterdam
TEL 31 20 4202021
FAX 31 20 4201152

Translated by Philip Jenkins, King's Lynn
Production: The Pepin Press, Amsterdam
Editorial assistant: Dorine van den Beukel

Printed in Singapore

Contents

Region **I**

Region **II**

CHILE

Region **III**

LA SERENA
Region **IV**   ● OVALLE

Region **V**   VALPARAÍSO
                SANTIAGO ●
A more detailed map   RANCAGUA ●
of Chile's wine regions   Region **VI**   SAN FERNANDO ●
can be found on   CURICÓ ●
page 76.   Region **VII**   TALCA ● LINARES ●
                                            ● CHILLÁN
                           CONCEPCIÓN ●
                           Region **VIII**

                           Region **IX**   ● TEMUCO

                           Region **X**
                                            PUERTO MONTT ●

                           Region **XI**

                           Region **XII**
                                            PUNTA ARENAS ●

                                                        4500 km

Foreword

Wine-growing has a long tradition in Chile. The first vines were planted in 1541 by Spanish conquistadores. However, centuries passed until the foundations were laid for quality-conscious wine-growing with European and above all French varieties around 1850. Slightly more than 10 years ago a new epoch dawned in Chilean wine-growing. Chile began to modernize its wine industry and to supply the world's most important export markets with modern wines in the international style.

Despite its long tradition of producing wine Chile numbers amongst the newcomers on the international wine scene. Nonetheless it has achieved phenomenal success in the USA, Canada and England in a very short space of time and in 1995 exported over 110 million bottles of wine. There is every chance that this figure will soon increase substantially, since there is scarcely a country which produces wines which are as good at Chilean prices.

It is not long ago that Chile has seen a wave of newly established small vineyards which focus on quality, the researching of new locations with great potential for growing wine and the consistent separation in production of good average wines from leading international ones. In many vineyards continuous development can be tasted with almost every successive vintage. I have therefore made every attempt to keep abreast of current developments in the full knowledge that a period of rapid change only admits of snapshots.

Without the support of Anette Diekmann this book would not have been possible. In Chile many vineyards and the two trade associations – Asociación de Exportadores y Embotelladores de Vino AG and ChileVid – have supported me in my researches. Douglas Murray and Virginia Fuenzalida deserve special thanks. In addition I would like to mention in gratitude Silvia Cava (ProChile Santiago), Susanne Friedrich (ProChile Bonn), and Hugo Calderón, the trade attaché at the Chilean embassy in Bonn, for their help in the realization of this book.

Jürgen Mathäss

Chile – The Distant Country

Desert, Tierra del Fuego, Andes and Sea

An unforgettable first impression of Chile is to be had by taking an aeroplane from Mendoza in Argentina to Santiago. The short, low flight over the Andes and down into the fertile valleys which extend to Santiago, offers grandiose views when visibility is clear. Just over the highest peaks of the Andes, which reach 7,000 m (23,000 ft) to the west and extending to the ocean, it is possible to see the narrow strip of land, 120 km (75 mls) wide, which forms Chile at this point.

At its widest Chile measures a mere 180 km (112 mls), but is just over 4,500 km (2,800 mls) long, the equivalent of the distance between Madrid and Moscow. The landscape is correspondingly varied, embracing the inhospitable beauty of the desert region in the North and the similarly inhospitable cold of Tierra del Fuego in the South. With a surface area of approximately 757,000 km² (292,000 sq mls), Chile is one of the smaller South American countries, whilst being three times as large as the United Kingdom in surface area. Outside of Greater Santiago, the country is divided into 12 numbered administrative regions, stretching from the Peruvian border in the North to Cape Horn in the South.

Sea, desert and the Andes have shaped the three northern regions (I-

PAGES 8-9: A country with countless geographical attractions. Lago Chungará (Region I) at 4,538 m (15,000 ft) is supposedly the highest lake in the world.
ABOVE: The Guallatiri church with the similarly named volcano in Region I.
PAGE 11 LEFT: The Lauca National Park is located near Putre, the northernmost point in Chile at a height of 4,500 m (15,000 ft).
PAGE 11 RIGHT: From Punta Arenas, Chile's southernmost city, many rewarding places can be visited, including Pinguinera in Otway Bay (Region XII).

III). In a stretch of land almost 1,200 km (745 mls) long, less than one million inhabitants live in a dry, wide landscape which is only occasionally interrupted by white churches and clay houses bleached by the sun. Particularly in the rural regions, it is still quite common to find that Indian dialects are mixed with Spanish, the country's official language. The few larger cities are located on the coast or near the Andes. Rich in mineral deposits, especially in copper, these northern regions make a considerable contribution to the prosperity of the country.

Large mountains dominate the region adjoining to the south (IV). The principle crop cultivated in fertile valleys such as Elqui or Limarí is that of vines for the production of pisco. La Serena, after Santiago the second oldest city in Chile and today a picturesque, well-tended city in the colonial style is the cradle of Chilean wine-growing. The first vines were already growing here in the 16th century.

Central Chile begins with the Valparaíso Region (V), and extends to Bío-Bío (VIII). It is here that by far the most people live – about 70 per cent of the entire population are concentrated in a stretch of land 500 km (310 mls) long. In very close proximity are to the found Valparaíso, the country's largest port, Viña del Mar, the largest holiday centre and Santiago, the dominating, pulsating capital with over four million people. The broad, fertile Central Valley which extends over the whole length of these four administrative regions offers the best conditions for agriculture and wine-growing. Its farmland is punctuated by eucalyptus trees, willows and poplars, particularly along the rivers and irrigation canals.

The cool, humid and green Chilean South begins with the bewitchingly beautiful lake area near Temuco (Region IX is called Araucanía). Up until 1880 the Araucanians, or Mapuche Indians, ruled the country's interior south of Bío-Bío. Since 1851 Germans have emigrated to this region with its quite beautiful landscape and have left their mark on the architecture, on regional specialities as well as forming isolated linguistic enclaves. To the south of Puerto Montt, the Andes, valleys and sea form an attractive, partially inaccessible landscape of islands, fjords, rivers and lakes, which extends to Tierra del Fuego (Regions X-XXI). Furthermore, part of Antarctica also belongs to Chile.

Santiago, with a population of 5 million at the foot of the Andes, is the centre of all economic and cultural activity.

The area between the Andean peaks and the bottom of the Pacific Ocean, 200 km (125 mls) away and 14,000 m (46,000 ft) lower down, is volcanically active. Earthquakes here have repeatedly caused considerable damage in many places and have destroyed historical buildings from the country's colonial past. Since there is a considerable amount of wood in the South, all larger towns in southern Chile are especially memorable for their beautiful wooden houses in the colonial style. When visiting vineyards in this region it is sometimes possible to admire country houses built with wood, which have been restored at some expense.

The People

South America is culturally quite diverse. Any uniformity would be
undermined immediately by the fact that the continent embraces very
different climatic zones. The three southerly states Uruguay,
Argentina and Chile are undoubtedly regarded as being more
European than other South American countries. However, even
between these countries, and above all between Chile and Argentina,
there are considerable differences of mentality and a mutual antipa-
thy which is nonetheless expressed in cordial terms.

In Chile, German, British and for the most part Spanish immigrants
formed much more of a cohesive whole with the original Indian population than had happened in neighbouring countries. A very distinc-
tive national feeling came into existence, which also resulted from
the economic interests of the upper classes. Chileans as a people can
be described as having the following qualities: ambition, toughness,

single-mindedness but also a cautious sense of reserve, exceptional politeness and a willingness to learn. The Chileans have even been described on occasions as the Prussians of South America. In fiercely fought wars with neighbouring countries Bolivia and Peru, in particular during the War of the Pacific (1879-83), Chile was able to extend its borders by taking land rich in commodities.

Out of a total population of 14 million inhabitants one-third lives in Santiago de Chile, the lively, multifaceted capital. The architecture of the capital, which is in the style of a large European city, increasing prosperity and international flair provide a contrast with the colourful country people, Indian cultural elements and the cultural legacy of a clash between rich and poor. Santiago is the capital of a centralized state. All economic and political aspects of life converge in what is by far the largest city in Chile – cities such as Valparaíso, Viña del Mar and Concepción only have around 300,000 inhabitants each.

Economy

Chile is rich in mineral resources. It possesses the largest copper deposits in the world. The mining of iron ore and the extraction of saltpetre are also of great importance. Fishing is also an important industry along the extensive coast. Apart from fishing and mining, agricultural products, above all fresh fruit, raisins, preserved fruit and wine make a considerable contribution to exports.

For decades the unfair division of land (75 per cent is owned in the form of large estates) and the substantial gap between rich and poor have shaped the country's politics and also its economic development. This social conflict has still not been resolved. However, for

LEFT AND BELOW: Fresh fruit as well as wine is one of the most important exports for Chilean agriculture.

With its rich mineral deposits Chile belongs to the privileged countries of the world. Copper exports account for more than 40 per cent of export income. Chuquicamata (left) is the largest copper mine in the world.

several years the country has profited from an economy which has become stable and which is tremendously oriented towards growth. This has led to a clear improvement in the economic situation. Chile today is the most successful country in South America from an economic point of view.

With the end of the Pinochet dictatorship political and economic restraints also disappeared, the currency became more stable, exports rose and a greater level of prosperity was established. The gross national product has grown in the last ten years by over 80 per cent. The German newspaper *Die Zeit* has observed that wherever the pulse of the Chilean economic miracle is measured the indicators are optimistic, citing a surplus on the trade balance, one of the lowest levels of inflation on the subcontinent, ever increasing record investment, currency reserves for an entire year of imports, and the virtual absence of earlier debt problems. The middle classes are growing and are intensifying the economic development of the country in hand with dynamic companies, for which Chile is already famous in South America. With the development of the economy environmental problems are increasing, above all around the capital city Santiago. Here an effort is presently being made to overcome the smog with stricter legislation on exhaust fumes. However, one-third of the population live beneath the poverty line. The insufficient minimum wages of the workers, agricultural workers and smallholders may support the international competitiveness of the Chilean export economy, but do not even secure the minimal living requirements of their recipients. Even Chilean businessmen are today of the view that the social problems arising from the minimum wages paid are the country's most pressing. The wine industry also contributed to the economic boom which began after 1985. Connoisseurs have for a long time seen great potential in Chilean vineyards. It is true, however, that Cabernet

Sauvignon, Merlot, Chardonnay and Sauvignon Blanc have only been sold internationally for a few years. Previously the Chilean wine industry almost exclusively produced wine for domestic consumption.

Travelling and Chile

The journey to Chile by aeroplane is quite simple. More than twenty airlines fly to Santiago. There is no need for a tourist visa. By land there is only one connection from north to south, the Pan-American Highway, and a few passes in the Andes. It is possible to travel around by overland bus for long distances in comfort, however, when travelling in this way it is rather difficult to visit the vineyards which are slightly out of the way. To visit the bodegas it is advisable to rent a car with a driver in case one has an insufficient knowledge of the language. English is also spoken at the Wine Export Association in Santiago de Chile (Tel. 56 2 2342503, Fax 2311706), and help is available in organising visits to bodegas. The travel bureau Turismo Cocha maintains an office at the airport.

Santiago has a wide selection of hotels, ranging from the luxurious Sheraton which is in a quiet and relatively central location (Tel. 56 2 2335000, Fax 2341729) and other five-star hotels (Kempinski, Crown-Plaza, Carrera, Galerías) to the quiet, small, but very well-maintained Bidasoa (Tel. 56 2 2421525, Fax 2289798). The latter is popular with foreign travellers who are interested in the country's wine. Outside of the capital smaller hotels can always be found along the Pan-American Highway or in the cities.

No visitor to Chile need forego good food. Typical and traditional dishes are *asados* (barbecued meat), which can be enjoyed with live folklore at Los Buenos Muchachos (Ricardo Camming 1031), seafood, *empanadas* (stuffed dough pasties which are served as a snack) or corn dishes such as *humitas* or *pastel de choclo*. Santiago has also overtaken most capital cities in South America with its gourmet restaurants. Exceptionally good and pleasant are the restaurants El Suizo (Vitacura 3285, Tel. 56 2 2083603) and the Entre Ríos (Las Condes 10.480, Tel. 56 2 2171963) which has an attractive garden. El Balcón (Valentin Letelier 1339, Tel. 56 2 6992582) is a popular lunchtime rendezvous for people from the world of politics and commerce. A popular area for the evening is the artists' quarter Bellavista where one can enjoy food, dancing, cabaret or simply a glass of beer in one of the many street bars.

Chile is one of the safest and most uncomplicated countries in which to travel in South America. There are no tropical diseases, although it is advisable when staying for a longer period to be inoculated against typhoid and hepatitis B. Nearly all common medicines are available. When walking in the streets and after parking a car the normal precautions against theft are sufficient.

Wine in Chile

ABOVE: Pedro de Valdivia conquered the Mapuche Indians in 1540-41 and thereby created the preconditions for the founding of the city of Santiago.

Throughout many books about wine and specialist journals, wine writers from America, England and other European countries can be found enthusing about the great potential of Chile as a wine-producing country. In fact Chilean wine-growing still has much further to go before it exhausts its scope for development. The reliable climate in the protected Central Valley, the different types of soils and microclimates in the side valleys, modern vine varieties grown on their own rootstock which are free of phylloxera, the competitive, highly modern wineries and the ambitious wine-makers offer the best conditions which wine connoisseurs the world over could wish for. That this development should only manifest itself over the last ten years is the result of the history of Chile and its wines.

From the First Vines to Modern Wine-growing

It was a habit amongst the Ancient Greeks, who were keen travellers, to bring their own vines with them, wherever they settled far from home. It is easier to cultivate wine on the spot than it is to transport it for weeks on end by ship. This is probably how wine cultivation began in the Rhône valley and on the Iberian peninsula.
The Spanish and Portuguese were no different two thousand years later. It was the conquistadores who planted the first vines in South America. They were principally interested in enriching themselves with the treasures that were to be had without delay, and if necessary by force. They were soon followed by settlers, who came to the New World to become farmers and large landowners.
The history of the Americas as a wine-growing continent – it is

claimed – is said to have begun with one of the cruellest conquistadores. Hernando Cortés, the conqueror of the Aztec empire, is supposed to have given the horrifying order that for every hundred Indians that were killed, a thousand vines should be planted. That was in the year 1524. It was soon after the scarcely less bloody conquest of the Inca empire by Francisco Pizarro that the first vineyards were planted in what is Chile today. In 1540-41 Pedro de Valdivia defeated the Araucanian Indians to the south of the old Inca empire and founded Santiago. At this time the colonization of what is now the North of Chile as well as wine-growing in Chile began, and shortly afterwards the former conquistador Francisco de Aguirre planted the first vineyards to the north of Santiago at La Serena. Diego de Oro also planted vines near Santiago.

Wine-growing was originally dependent upon the País grape, a variety which provides a substantial crop. País was described as a lowly, dark grape by the Jesuit Father Alonso Ovalle, who also reported the use of the Torontel, Albilho, Muscatel and Mollar grape varieties. These still exist today for the most part. Of all grapes pressed in every Chilean grape harvest one-third are of the País variety.

Wine-growing certainly got off to a good start given the optimal climatic conditions, but there were setbacks of another kind. Indians, who refused to admit defeat in Chile for hundreds of years would rebel, time and again destroying the wine-growing infrastructure in less heavily populated regions. The first exports to other colonies failed more because of the difficult conditions under which they were transported than because of any lack of demand. An example of this was the seizure in 1578 by Sir Francis Drake of a Spanish ship carrying over 1700 wineskins from Chile to Peru.

The uninterrupted development of wine-growing over the following three centuries was only possible in the region around Santiago. This was because of unrest amongst the Mapuches, who even into the nineteenth century regularly brought wine-growing to a halt with widespread destruction of vineyards in the South, up to a distance of about 150 km (93 mls) from Santiago. There was a considerable increase in the area of vines under cultivation in the seventeenth century, despite the wars with the Mapuches. King Philip II of Spain even issued an edict, forbidding the planting of new grapes, in order to protect Spanish wine-growers from irksome competition. Although today its vines are dedicated to growing table grapes and grapes for the manufacture of pisco, the Atacama region was also known for its wines. In the ensuing years Chile increasingly emerged as an exporter of cheap wine in large volumes, thus causing annoyance amongst Spanish wine-growers. In 1774 the Spanish king forbade by decree the export of Chilean wines to other Spanish colonies, in particular Mexico. Simple wines sweetened with a thickened must remained typical for the unassuming bodegas in the Andean colony until the middle of the nineteenth century. By 1830 Chile had become

independent. In that year, Claude Gay persuaded government offi-
cials to set up an agricultural research institute, where seventy international grape varieties were soon planted. Silvestre Ochagavía
brought the first French vines to Chile in 1851 and cultivated them.
His example was followed by men such as Antonio Tocornal, Macario
Ossa, Maximiano Errázuriz, Luis Cousiño and others. This marked the
beginning of the growing of modern quality wines in Chile. The
founders of the bodegas which were mostly French in their orienta-
tion, also imported wine-makers from France as well as the requisite
technology. It became fashionable for the aristocracy, and those
Chileans who had become wealthy through their mining interests, to
possess a vineyard which was run by Frenchmen. Several of the
bodegas which were founded between 1850 and 1890, Concha y
Toro, Errázuriz, Santa Carolina, Cousiño Macul, Santa Rita, Tarapacá
and San Pedro still dominate the Chilean wine industry today.

When the phylloxera aphid caused terrible damage in Europe from
1860 onwards, modern wine-growing in Chile soon became a prof-

itable export business. In the year 1900 there were already 40,000 ha (100,000 a) of vines under cultivation in Chile. This figure grew substantially in subsequent years, reaching 80,000 ha (200,000 a) by 1930 and 102,000 ha (252,000 a) by 1938. This trend was halted partly because of new legislation concerning alcohol, which prohibited the planting of new vines, and partly because of the Second World War, which isolated Chile to a considerable extent. The restrictive government policy on alcohol continued after the war, and wine was treated by the state as a necessary evil.

From the Great Crisis into a Golden Future

The acreage under cultivation remained constant at around 106,000 ha (262,000 a) until the end of the 1970s. As long as sales continued to flourish in the domestic market there appeared to be no obligation to bring wine-growing and cellar technology up to standards prevailing internationally.

However, when in business, to be complacent and assume that current levels of profit will be sustained of their own accord in the future, is often to court disaster. The healthy profitability which the wine industry had enjoyed for decades had made the estate owners carefree and comfortable. Once restrictions on wine-growing were abolished in the 1970s, the wine-growers increased production substantially, in spite of the fact that domestic consumption had sunk dramatically from an earlier level of 50 litres (13.2 gal) per head to less than half (today the figure stands at 11 litres/2.9 gal) and the export market barely existed. The entire production was used for domestic wines, table grapes and pisco, the national drink.

In both 1982 and 1983 the Chilean harvest was of over 6 million hectolitres (160 m gal) of wine, more than they had ever made before. The result was an enormous glut, which finally precipitated a crisis in the wine industry. Grape and wine prices sank beneath production costs and the wineries, which had been spoilt for profits, went into loss. Those managing the wine industry recognized that they were set on a catastrophic course unless they could gain access to the world market. Thanks to a Chilean characteristic, something which neighbouring countries are sometimes a little uncomfortable with – a sense of ambition which remains unmatched in South America – the leading producers changed course. They made an enormous investment in bringing virtually the entire industry up to modern standards prevailing

PAGE 22 ABOVE: The Jesuit father Alonso Ovalle (left) was the first to report the use of the País, Torontel and Muscatel grape varieties in Chile, the conquistador Francisco de Aguirre (centre) planted the first vines in Chile, and Don Silvestre Ochagavía (right) brought the first modern French vines to Chile in 1851.
PAGE 22 BELOW: *Noche Buena* – Lively Christmas celebrations with wine, music and dance in 1872.

worldwide in less than five years – something which had never been achieved before by a wine-producing country. Several vineyards with 10,000 ha (25,000 a) were cleared or were switched to the production of table grapes. During the last ten years the surface area devoted to the cultivation of table grapes has risen from 35,000 to 49,800 ha (87,000 to 123,000 a), whilst the total area dedicated to producing wine was slimmed down from 67,000 to 54,000 ha (166,000 to 133,000 a) during the same period. Taking their lead in particular from the investments that Miguel Torres had made in his estate, which for the time was spectacularly modern, the wineries sent their specialist staff abroad for further training, bought the latest technology and acquired the necessary know-how. In practical terms the wine industry was beginning all over again. Within a few years one-third of every vintage was being sold abroad.

The centralized structure of the vineyards made this economic revolution possible, as only ten large wineries bottle more than eighty per cent of all Chilean wine. The situation is similar to that of a hunderd years ago, in that most bodegas belong to families from the Chilean financial aristocracy. For these families wine-growing is not their only source of income. They could afford to modernize an entire industry. Enormous amounts of money flowed into vineyards, modern presses, temperature regulated stainless steel tanks and barriques. Young wine-makers were sent to leading American and European concerns in order to continue their education and respected oenologists were brought into the country from successful wine-producing regions. Wines which were to the taste of the modern, international buying public were being produced and marketed at extraordinary speed. Since 1990 the word in wine circles has been of excellent, modern, Chilean wines and their extraordinarily attractive prices.

Outside Investors

Chile is now attracting considerable amounts of foreign capital as a wine-producing nation, because the Chileans have proved that money can be made when growing conditions are excellent and labour and land costs are relatively low. It is above all the French, who in general have a very good understanding of *terroir*, quality and wine-making, who are particularly interested in Chilean wine. Lafite-Rothschild (with Los Vascos), Cos d'Estournel (with Aquitania), William Fèvre (Fèvre Chile), Larose Trintaudon (Casas del Toqui), Massenez (Santa Amalia), Grand Marnier (Casa Lapostolle/Domaine Rabat) and Henri Marionnet (TerraNoble) all operate in Chile with wholly-owned subsidiaries or have substantial investments. The situation prevailing is rather different to that of the last century when the Chilean founders of vineyards would increase their standing by retaining French wine-makers. Today French investors purchase entire wineries in Chile.

For several years the surface area of vines under cultivation has been increasing, whilst grape prices had been rising up to two years ago. Both are closely related. In the past many large wineries have barely possessed any vineyards of their own and covered their requirements by purchasing grapes, must or wine. Now they are cultivating their own vineyards, not only to be independent of the grape farmers and their prices, but also to do justice to the increased demand for better wines by having proprietary vineyards, since the main interest for those selling grapes lies in achieving high vineyard yields.

New plantings in the old, traditional regions do not always flourish. Whilst wine-growing terrain used almost to be selected on the basis

BELOW: Many of the bodega buildings erected at the time of the onset of 'French' wine-growing in Chile are still standing. It is however rare to find treasure-chambers with old vintages, such as those found here at Cousiño Macul.

of 'the warmer the better', the wine which is produced there is heavy, rich in alcohol and often somewhat rough. New and cooler locations are being developed, to be able to cater in particular for the international trend towards fresher and more elegant white wines.

Chile and Europe: Each to his Own

Anyone familiar with Chilean wines in Europe and who is travelling in Chile must be prepared for surprises. Wines which are familiar abroad are only rarely available. The Vinoteca in the Hotel Radisson (Vitacura 2610) maintains a small, but excellent selection of export wines. Wines produced for the home market mostly have a different taste, and are often a disappointment to Europeans. The fashion in Europe and North America was for fresh, fruity wines with a moderate alcohol content which have not been barrelled for too long, but rather kept briefly in new barriques. Concentrating on the world market, the wineries had to address this taste and make a fundamental change in the way in which wine had been made for decades. Domestic production, which still accounts for two-thirds of all wine made, has since then been virtually of secondary importance. The wineries certainly have to follow a dual-track policy. The production of the entire Chilean wine industry is divided into wines for the domestic market and those made for export. Nearly all of the older wineries which were in existence before 1985 offer both types of wine. By contrast, most bodegas which were newly founded in the wake of the crisis are working exclusively for the export market. The two types of wine could scarcely be more different. The latter-day wines made for export have clear varietal flavours and a fruity elegance. The better-quality wines have a hint of vanilla thanks to the

newer wood used in oaking. Wines made for export require low temperatures for fermentation and will not tolerate any exposure to air. They require complicated technology in the cellar, and lower vineyard yields are necessary to produce the better wines. 'International' grape varieties such as Chardonnay, Sauvignon Blanc, Merlot and Cabernet Sauvignon, as well as Pinot Noir, Riesling and Gewürztraminer where possible are required here. By contrast, a large part of the domestic wine market is supplied from high-yielding vineyards producing up to 25 tonness per hectare (10 tons per acre) of the old and less highly regarded grape varieties. Such wines taste oxidized and oldish, instead of displaying the freshness and fruitiness of the varietal export wines. Even white wines for the home market are rarely consumed less than three years after harvesting. I myself, perhaps with the exception of the *Las Encinas* of San Pedro have almost never found a domestic white wine which I would like to drink. Red wines produced for the home market are reminiscent of traditional Spanish wines from Jumilla or Valencia. Such wines can be very attractive, if one is partial to this style. Admittedly, the large wineries did attempt to make the international style popular in Chile itself. This has failed hitherto, less because of price and more because it goes against the traditional Chilean taste in wine. Even the success in the export market was initially regarded with indifference. Chileans like their wine to be as it always was. Why indeed should tastes be the same the world over?

It is not even 15 years ago that the opening up of the world market took place. Even the everyday domestic wines, which taste oxidized to the European palate, fulfil in their own way verifiable standards of quality. Every larger bodega is fitted out with a well-equipped laboratory which is run by knowledgeable staff.

Climate, Soil and Grape Varieties

Grapevines grow almost everywhere. Ten thousand year old seeds have been found frozen in Siberia and vineyards have even been planted near the Equator. Good wines however do not grow everywhere. Dry, warm (but not too warm) summers with substantial temperature changes between day and night, cool winters, a low exposure to wind, stony soil and an altogether not too copious supply of water are all things that wine-growers require for their vineyards, in

PAGES 28-29: Modern trellis systems, international grape varieties and extremely well-suited *terroir* form the basis for the success registered by Chile in the export market over the last decade.
ABOVE: País, the grape variety from Chile's colonial past, is still quite widespread.
BELOW: In the newly laid out vineyards most vine varieties are international ones.

order to be able to harvest healthy, full-bodied grapes. Slightly more water and rich soil will provide large amounts of fruit of an ordinary quality under otherwise similar conditions. Each approach has its uses and both find ideal circumstances in Chile.

There is scarcely another country with better conditions for producing wine than Chile. The climate and soils in a wine-growing region a good 500 km (310 mls) in length are broadly similar to those of the Californian Napa Valley or – according to location – the areas between Southern Spain and Burgundy, where the climate is less reliable. Protected from the raw ocean winds and supplied with water from melted Andean snow, Chilean wine-growers are able to cultivate vines in a variety of microclimates. Some are suited to fresh, fruity wines, others to powerful, ripe red and white wines. Yet others make it possible to produce large amounts of everyday table wines.

Climate

Chile is a strip of land 4,500 km (2,800 mls) long with an approximate average width of a mere 180 km (112 mls). Of these, at best 130 km (80 mls) can be used for the country's infrastructure or for agricultural purposes, because the Andes, which rise up to as high as 7,000 m (23,000 ft) to the east, and border Chile throughout its entire length, render part of the country inaccessible. To the west, the Pacific Ocean forms a natural border. In the South there is a large, virtually uninhabited Arctic region and in the North lies the Atacama desert.

The landscape and the climate for wine-growing is shaped by another mountain chain, this time a coastal one, the Cordillera de la Costa or Coastal Range, which rises up to a height of 2,000 m (6,600 ft). Between the Andes and the Coastal Range, a large valley stretches virtually throughout the whole of Chile, in which are to be found the principal areas of land available for agriculture. The valley is traversed from east to west by river valleys, which carry water from the melted snows of the Andes to the sea. This water, which is rich in minerals, is used for watering land under cultivation, since the country's rainfall is not equal to the task. Between the Aconcagua Valley, approximately 150 km (95 mls) north of Santiago and the city of Chillán, 400 km (250 mls) to the south of the capital, grapes are cultivated in a Mediterranean climate for the manufacture of wine. The Coastal Range keeps the sea sufficiently at bay from the valley which lies behind it, but allows just enough moist sea air in along its transverse valleys, so that the summers do not become too hot. The summers are always dry, and the annual rainfall of 350 to 800 mm (14 to 32 in) occurs almost exclusively in the winter months.

The climate in the North tends to be warmer and the region enjoys less rainfall, whilst in the South it is cooler and more humid.

Propitious alluvial soil, loam, clay, gravel subsoil, rubble which has come down from the Andes and lime in several locations can often vary within the smallest space – the best conditions for growing the most varied grape varieties.

However, according to each individual location and the proximity of rivers or the Andes, there is a great variety of microclimates. One of the most noted exceptions is the cool Casablanca Valley between Santiago and Valparaíso. Locations near the Andes, above all those higher ones between 500 and 1,000 m (1,600 and 3,300 ft), are exposed to stronger variations in temperature thanks to the cold air which descends from the mountains at night. These locations produce wines with a better structure.

Soil

The soil in which the grapes grow has a fundamental effect on the character of a wine. The slate soils along the Moselle, the coarse gravel soils of the Médoc and the limestone locations used for the Grand Cru in Burgundy have made their wines famous. And it is not by chance that wholly different grape varieties grow in these soils, since tried and trusted grape varieties are also very much a part of the success enjoyed by these wine-producing regions.

Soils which are well aired, are easily heated, not too moist and absorb water easily always produce the best wines. And soils which are full of nutrients encourage growth. It is precisely the stony soils which are often too barren for ordinary agricultural purposes which may provide these conditions.

The large Central Valley is characterized by alluvial land containing sediment, stone and minerals, which has been carried down for thousands of years into the valley by the rivers descending from the

Andes. Often the soils go very deep, but since irrigation is extensive the vines form only comparatively shallow roots as a rule.

Apart from these predominantly alluvial soils, there are soils to be found with a loam and clay content in the Maipo region, as well as in Rapel and Cachapoal. Individual locations with tuffaceous deposits in Rapel and Maule produce elegant, filigreed wines. Just as interesting from the point of view of structure are the wines which come from the volcanic soils to the south of Curicó and in the southernmost region Bío-Bío. Rich and heavy soils, some even having a muddy and boggy consistency can be found to a certain extent on the eastern slopes of the coastal mountains and in the region of Bío-Bío. These soils are only suitable for the production of simple bulk wines.

The Absence of Phylloxera

There is one aspect of Chilean soil which cannot be overemphasized sufficiently. This has nothing to do with rock formations, but involves an insect. The phylloxera aphid, which at the end of the last century destroyed virtually all wine-growing areas in the world, has spared Chile hitherto. For this reason the vines which grow in the country's vineyards are still clones growing on their original rootstocks, which it has long been impossible to grow in Europe.

World-wide, the species of vine known as *Vitis vinifera*, to which practically all vines used internationally belong, have to be grafted on to North American roots, which cannot be harmed by the root sucking insect. But in Chile, Cabernet Sauvignon, Merlot, Chardonnay and other vines have been spared. Many specialists regard this fact as being of the highest importance, as they make the assumption that vines change their character when they have to be grafted on to 'other' roots.

Why was Chile so fortunate in this respect? Reference is often made to the country's geographical remoteness from other areas. It seems more logical however to assume that the regular flooding of the vineyards for irrigation purposes restricted the advance of the phylloxera. Even today, flooding with mineral-rich river water from the melted snows of the Andes is the normal method of irrigation. The perfect system of channels which had already been partly built by the Incas, functions mostly without pumps. It operates on the simple basis of opening sluice-gates where irrigation is required. The drawback with this system of irrigation is that valuable soil is washed away. Whilst modernizing vineyards with drip irrigation limits erosion, it may also open the door for phylloxera to come to Chile.

Grape Varieties

An exact identification of grape varieties first became important in
Chile when the focus of the wine industry moved towards the world
market. In many old vineyards the mixture of different varieties
which it was previously customary to plant still exists today and the
exact proportions between these different varieties are often not
known at all. The official statistics can therefore only give an indication rather than any meticulously accurate information.

At present the official statistics for Chile show that the entire area of
grapevines under cultivation stands at 113,581 ha (281,000 a). Of
these, 49,803 ha (123,000 a) are for table grapes, 9,385 ha (23,190 a)
are for the production of pisco and 54,393 ha (134,405 a) are for the
production of wine.

The old pergola system has one advantage for those who harvest the grapes. It provides shade and avoids the need for working whilst bending over. Because of a high yield the grapes are often more suitable for everyday wines.

Red Wine Varieties

País

This traditional vine is the most widely cultivated in Chile today; origin unknown; dates from the country's colonial period; different variations of it can be found throughout the whole of the Americas (in Argentina it is known as *Criolla*, in California as *Mission*); produces large harvest; simple, rustic red wines; not used for exported wines.

Cabernet Sauvignon

This grape variety from Bordeaux has made triumphant progress throughout the world and today can be found wherever great red wines are made: California, Australia, Italy etc.; is currently regarded as the best red wine variety in the world; present in Chile for approximately 150 years, vines still grow on own rootstock; requires a warm climate, low yields and well-ripened grapes (otherwise a grassy flavour obtrudes); fruity, strong wine rich in tannin with a blackcurrant bouquet, as well as one of eucalyptus in Chile.

Merlot

The mellower of the two great Bordeaux varieties lacks the pronounced flavour of other better quality red wines; cast as its 'smaller brother', Merlot is to be found alongside Cabernet wherever it goes; often – as in Bordeaux – blended with Cabernet; in Chile already the second most important of the fine red grape varieties; the grapes have thin skins, and therefore a tendency to rot; vines can produce a lot of fruit, which results in ordinary wines.

Pinot Noir

The noble Pinot Noir of Burgundy is difficult in both cellar and vineyard and makes great demands on the place it is grown, but when it is successful it produces one of the very great wines of the world; mellow and velvety with a captivating, slightly sweet cherry bouquet; requires a temperate climate and likes limestone soils; not very widespread in Chile, but planted often as an experiment – up to now without great results; a tradition for Undurraga.

Malbec (also known as *Cot*)

One of the earlier Bordeaux varieties (still of importance in Cahors), which has taken root above all in Argentina; in small yields can produce powerful, dark wines; in Chile, rarely in evidence as a varietal wine, e.g. Cánepa and La Fortuna; decline in amount cultivated perhaps due to grape's sensitivity to a number of factors.

White Wine Varieties

Sauvignon Blanc

Next to Chardonnay this is the most popular grape variety internationally for better quality white wines, and comes from the Loire (Sancerre!) and from Bordeaux (used for white Bordeaux, though mostly blended with Semillon there); in cool locations develops a typical gooseberry bouquet and has high acidity – as in the Loire; when grown in a warm climate is less well-defined, the alcohol content is higher and it is then largely intended for barrique ageing – as in Bordeaux or California; in Chile both versions are present in modern wines; long tradition of cultivation, but in most Chilean vineyards the inferior Sauvignonasse, which has a weaker aroma, prevails over the true Sauvignon Blanc, so that in contrast to other grape varieties it is the younger plantings of true Sauvignon which provide the most typical varietal wines.

Moscatel de Alejandría

This is one of the oldest of the many different types of Muscat grape; previously found in North Africa, there are still large areas under cultivation in Spain; provides good yields of grapes with a high sugar content, which is otherwise rather weak in aroma; often used as drying and table grapes, as is also the case in Chile, where the grape is very suitable for pisco; still the second most important variety for wine production, exclusively used for wines for the home market.

Chardonnay

Regarded as one of the best white wine grapes and at present probably the most popular in the world; found in practically every country; easily recognizable as a great wine and enjoys enormous popularity; has a neutral bouquet which can range from melon to the exotic and good acidity; excellent for barrique ageing; originally made famous by the great white Burgundies of Chablis, Meursault and Montrachet; best cultivated in limestone soils, generally not very difficult to cultivate, but only under good conditions, namely in low yields in a climate which is not too hot, will it produce high-quality grapes; previously almost absent from Chile, then the vine which showed the strongest growth; constant new plantings, now above all in cooler regions such as Casablanca.

Semillon

Made famous by dry, white Bordeaux and Sauternes, in both cases usually blended with Sauvignon Blanc; widespread in Australia and South America; on its own as a dry wine it is neutral, plump, low in acidity and somewhat uninteresting; previously very important in Chile; now strongly in decline and mainly used for domestic wines.

Torontel

This grape variety which originates from Galicia is still very widespread in Argentina; provides high yields of white wine, fully flavoured with Muscat and low in acid content; is used for simple wines for the home market and also partly for pisco.

Riesling

One of the finest white grape varieties with a broad spectrum of nuances in taste ranging from the light and dry to the sweet, very aromatic and high acid content; suitable above all for cultivation in cool locations; some attempts in Chile, used unblended amongst others by San Pedro, Santa Mónica, Santa Emiliana and Cánepa.

PAGES 38-39: Chardonnay (left) and Cabernet Sauvignon (right).

Grape Prices

Thanks to the great success in exports, the demand for modern varieties was consistently higher than supply for several years. Between 1987 and 1993, the price of grapes rose tenfold. It was only with the harvests of 1994 and 1995, when many new vines began to yield grapes, that it fell dramatically to less than half of the 1993 price. One kilogram of Chardonnay grapes cost about 17p (US$ 0.26) during the large harvest of 1995, whilst ordinary white grapes only cost slightly more than 4p (US$ 0.06).

A comparison between the years 1985 and 1996 shows the enormous change in the Chilean attitude to quality. The reduction in the area of vines under cultivation is exclusively related to the fact that virtually half of the simple red wine variety País and over one-third of the old white wine variety Moscatel de Alejandría were dug up. In exchange there were considerable plantings of modern, international vines. The proportion of grape varieties suitable for export rose within ten years by 10,000 ha (25,000 a) to 45 per cent of vines under cultivation in Chile.

Grape Varieties in Chile 1985 and 1996 (in ha)

	1985	1996	Change (%)
Red Varieties			
País	29,384	15,281	-48
Cabernet Sauvignon	8,134	12,233	51
Merlot	1,000	2,689	168
Carignan	875	532	-40
Cot (Malbeck)	941	402	-58
Tintorera	271	384	41
Cinsaut	236	178	-25
Pinot Noir	103	217	109
White Varieties			
Sauvignon Blanc	4,961	6,131	23
Moscatel de Alejandría	9,331	5,973	36
Chardonnay	245	4,379	1,690
Semillon	6,195	2,650	-58
Torontel	1,262	1,062	-16
Chasselas	834	406	-52
Riesling	277	297	7
Chenin Blanc	18	107	494
Others	3,065	1,286	-55
Total	67,132	54,300	-19

Distribution of Varieties by Region 1996 (in ha)

	Aconcagua (Casablanca)	Maipo	Rapel	Maule	Bío-Bío	Total
Red Varieties	344	3,460	6,008	16,219	6,156	32,187
País	63	5	351	9,120	5,742	15,281
Cabernet Sauvignon	146	3,047	4,399	4,504	137	12,233
Merlot	74	284	853	1,474	4	2,689
Carignan	1	5	6	420	100	532
Cot (Malbeck)	8	41	185	163	5	402
Tintorera	–	16	109	258	1	384
Cinsaut	–	–	–	77	101	178
Pinot Noir	39	45	74	57	2	217
Others	13	17	31	146	64	271
White Varieties	1,516	1,394	2,796	9,549	6,858	22,113
Sauvignon Blanc	169	386	867	4,599	110	6,131
Moscatel de Alejandría	–	40	20	220	5,693	5,973
Chardonnay	1,199	650	853	1,430	237	4,379
Semillon	23	135	716	1,689	87	2,650
Torontel	13	120	95	705	129	1,062
Chasselas	–	–	–	30	376	406
Riesling	13	45	89	112	38	297
Chenin Blanc	16	3	82	5	1	107
Others	83	15	64	759	187	1,108
Total	1,860	4,854	8,804	25,768	13,014	54,300

Source: Servicio Agrícola y Ganadero, Subdepartamento Alcoholes y Viñas, Santiago 1996

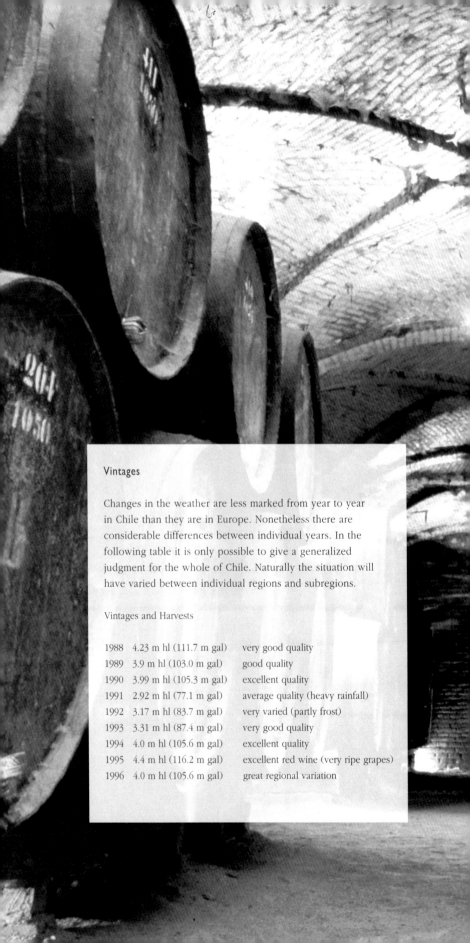

Vintages

Changes in the weather are less marked from year to year in Chile than they are in Europe. Nonetheless there are considerable differences between individual years. In the following table it is only possible to give a generalized judgment for the whole of Chile. Naturally the situation will have varied between individual regions and subregions.

Vintages and Harvests

1988	4.23 m hl (111.7 m gal)	very good quality
1989	3.9 m hl (103.0 m gal)	good quality
1990	3.99 m hl (105.3 m gal)	excellent quality
1991	2.92 m hl (77.1 m gal)	average quality (heavy rainfall)
1992	3.17 m hl (83.7 m gal)	very varied (partly frost)
1993	3.31 m hl (87.4 m gal)	very good quality
1994	4.0 m hl (105.6 m gal)	excellent quality
1995	4.4 m hl (116.2 m gal)	excellent red wine (very ripe grapes)
1996	4.0 m hl (105.6 m gal)	great regional variation

Wine-growing and Cellar Technology

As is the case in most wine-growing countries, the farms of Chile's rural areas are no exception in having their own vines. If the number of vines is sufficient and the farm has a cellar which is equipped even to a limited extent, the farm will produce its own wine and supply neighbours and relatives with it. Otherwise the grapes are delivered to one of the co-operatives, where they are processed into wine. The co-operatives bottle partly for some regional brands, but they sell much the largest part of their supply to the larger, private bodegas. This is the sector of Chilean agriculture where ordinary people play a role.

The other side of the coin is represented by the owners of large estates, in whose attractive houses servants maintain the grounds as well as preparing and serving the family's meals. In this prosperous group we find grape producers and suppliers of wine from the cask. Their land, rarely smaller than 100 ha (250 a) in size, is cultivated by farm workers and day-labourers whom they employ. The owners of large estates sell directly to the larger bodegas, often on long-term contracts, since as a rule they are in possession of good locations which produce valuable grapes. The bodegas would already like to exercise some influence on the vineyards according to their needs

RIGHT: Horses are more considerate than most tractor drivers towards vines, especially young vines. Many small farmers use them in preference to the machines on financial grounds.
BELOW: Irrigation still takes place in most vineyards along a branch system of channels using melted snow and ice, which is fed to the rows at certain times.

Much of the harvest is still picked by hand, above all because labour costs in Chile are lower than the cost of using many mechanical alternatives. However, in the large flat vineyards in the Central Valley, modern harvesting machinery can be used to good effect; the grape quality is uniform and selection virtually unnecessary.

during the course of the year. At present many new plantings are proving successful in the large estates. Since there is sufficient demand in the export market, investments in cellar equipment and a good oenologist are worthwhile.

The sale of grapes is an important point of contact in determining the quality of a wine. As long as certain grape varieties are sold mainly on a weight basis, the grape producers will be inclined to achieve as high a vineyard yield as possible, which is not beneficial to the quality of wine.

Once a considerable investment has been made in it, a vineyard will last for at least twenty years. It is precisely the old vines which produce the best grapes, even if not in large volumes. It is therefore not immediately possible to anticipate every fashionable change in the market by way of planting new vines. The vineyards were to a great extent laid out at a time when Chile made virtually no wines for export. Only in the case of Cabernet Sauvignon were Chilean winemakers in the position to draw immediately on old vines, from which it was possible to offer enough varietal wine for consumption on the world market. The situation had to be radically improved by means of regrafting and the planting of new vines. It is for this reason that one sees today many modern vineyards equipped with trellis systems which use wire frames, such as the lyre or cordon. Such vineyards can be up to twelve years old.

As well as modern trellis systems there are also countless *parronales*, a pergola system approximately two metres (two yards) high, which facilitates working by hand, helps to avoid frost and produces large yields.

Following the first wave of modernization, clones, rootstocks, vine age, soil conditions and microclimates are increasingly gaining in importance amongst the producers. As in other wine regions which concentrate on quality, each individual factor is optimized, for it is only then that the production of wines of world class is possible.

The sensitivity of wine-growers with regard to the irrigation of vineyards has also grown. About half of all vines under cultivation in Chile are regularly watered, as during the summer months there is very little rainfall. However, there is sufficient water available in the rivers, which is conveyed to the vineyards by means of a cleverly devised system of channels – mostly without pumps. This method of irrigation is advantageous in that the water requirements of the vineyards can be completely optimized. For decades, optimization

An uncomplicated grape harvest – unusually healthy and uniformly ripened grapes by European standards make work in the cellars easier.

As there are international standards of cellar technology for the four standard grape varieties of Cabernet Sauvignon, Chardonnay, Merlot and Sauvignon Blanc. which dominate exports and with which virtually every producer works, there is no specifically Chilean variation.

Fruity white wines
Separation of the must before cool, slow fermentation (14-17°C/57-63°F) and avoidance of any contact with air, no contact with wood.

Oaked white wines
Fermentation in barriques with more or less malolactic fermentation following alcoholic fermentation; ambient or cultured yeasts according to the policy of the winery; 3-8 months of maturation in barriques with the yeast.

Fruity, young red wines
Fermentation with skins, some pips and bits of stem, fermentation temperature of 23-26°C (73-79°F), not barrique aged.

Oaked red wines
Longer fermentation with skins, some pips and bits of stem; fermentation temperature of 26-30°C (79-86°F), aged in old and new oak.

ABOVE: Undurraga uses large barrels to mature its classic red wines.
LEFT: To produce fruity modern varietal wines there is scarcely a better container than the stainless steel tank, such as this one at the Carmen vineyard.

certainly meant the highest possible production of grapes. At high temperatures and with copious irrigation some vineyards still manage to produce 25 tonnes per hectare (10 tons per acre) easily. However, from such a yield nothing more than an ordinary, everyday wine is to be expected. To create high-quality wines, the amount of water must be reduced and a new optimal crop defined. An example would be a maximum of 8,000 kg (18,000 lb) of small Chardonnay grapes with an alcohol potential of 13 per cent and a specified level of wine acidity.

Those vines which are not watered are usually old ones located on a hillside with grape varieties which are only used for table wine. Whilst average yields for irrigated plots are around 12 tonnes per hectare (5 tons per acre), the unwatered sites achieve only about 4 tonnes per hectare (1.6 tons per acre).

In the shortest space of time it was possible to install all of the technology necessary for taking delivery of the grapes, pressing them, fermentation, storage and bottling, in order to process the grape harvest in the optimal fashion. Since the process of modernization first began in the year 1985, when the Cánepa winery followed the groundbreaking example of Torres, today's technology is largely of the most modern kind. As in all modern wine-making regions of the world, gleaming stainless steel tanks and storage cellars for barriques, enormous, cooled storage cellars and the most protective presses are

currently used at nearly all of the Chilean wineries that export their wines.

Mechanization was certainly taken too far at the beginning. But wine-makers soon learnt that too much movement damages the wine, too great a degree of separation of white wine must removes flavours and exaggerated fining and filtration measures destroy the character of wine. Today Chilean wine-makers work together with foreign advisers and are careful to follow the latest international trends.

As a rule, plastic containers are used for the grape harvest for wines of a better quality, although it is still possible to see lorries that rattle through the autumn sun for miles, piled high with grapes. The wine's acidity is then corrected at the crushing stage. Virtually all wineries that export have the equipment to store wine at low temperatures and to bottle in a sterile environment.

LEFT: Bottling as well as fermentation technology was brought to perfection. Prime concerns are sterilization and avoiding any oxidization.
BELOW: In modern bottling plants every single bottle is checked for clarity and perfect bottling.

What Do Chilean Wines Taste Like?

Since taste is always such a subjective issue, I shall limit myself here to providing the framework for a comparison with the wines of other countries.

Chilean export wines are practically always dry, although the production of sweet wines is also regulated by law. There are no clearly defined differences between the different levels of quality where wine is concerned, although specific wine regions have been established and their use on the label regulated. On the other hand, different levels of quality have come to play a role at export-oriented bodegas. These are firstly everyday wines with no indication of grape variety; medium-quality wines with a specified grape variety; a higher level where the words *Gran* or *Reserva* are used, mostly for barrique aged wines. At the larger bodegas wines of these differing levels of quality are usually given different brand names.

Is it possible to recognize Chilean wines from their bouquet and flavour in a blind tasting? This is most likely to be the case where a typical Chilean Cabernet Sauvignon is concerned. This grape variety is today already producing wines which have a characteristically Chilean bouquet. For it is only in the case of Cabernet Sauvignon that there were sufficiently old and 'mature' vines to be able to display the characteristic features of location and climate. Most Chilean Cabernets for the slightly more discerning palate are full-flavoured with an unusual component which is popularly described as eucalyptus. This suits some palates more than others. At any rate, with a little practice it is possible to recognize Chilean Cabernets easily from it.

If grown in a dedicated vineyard in moderate heat, Sauvignon Blanc can develop an exotic haziness in Chile, something which has been made famous by the New Zealand Sauvignons which have been so successful recently. However, one cannot rely on finding this characteristic, since there are still very few Sauvignons of this kind in Chile. Many come from old vineyards with a high proportion of Sauvignonasse, which has a rather neutral bouquet.

The limits to which it is possible to describe Chilean wine are very quickly reached, for the country's modern history of wine-growing only goes back ten years. In this short time producers have adapted themselves extraordinarily quickly to the world market. In particular, they are offering exactly those four standard grape varieties which have been in demand for years world-wide: Cabernet Sauvignon, Merlot, Chardonnay and Sauvignon Blanc. In comparison with wines of a similar quality from other countries, the Chilean product almost invariably represents much better value. Herein lies the secret of Chile's success.

There is scarcely one professional taster who would be able to recognize a Chardonnay costing between £3.50 and £8.50 (US$5.50 and US$13.00) as Chilean, South African or Australian. With few exceptions, this is generally quite difficult where modern overseas wine made with popular grape varieties is concerned. The phrase 'international style' is not an empty one. In the case of Chardonnay, for example, it can range anywhere in the world from an aromatic unoaked wine with a slightly higher acidity to a heavy, buttery, barrique fermented one in the Meursault style.

In order to develop wines which are unmistakable in character, more than ten years are necessary. Chile has the potential in the next twenty years to pick the best locations, the best clones and the individual technologies which are best suited to them. The first signs are there. On the strength of many details it was clear to see that with every vintage between 1990 and 1996 the level of quality was consistently on the increase. Over the next few years it seems more than likely that tasters in Chile's export markets will be increasingly hard pressed to keep up with the ever improving wines of Chile.

The Wine Regions

There are five legally defined wine-growing regions: Atacama, Coquimbo, Aconcagua, Valle Central (Central Valley) and Región del Sur (Southern Region). These regions with their subregions, as well as local areas, have been legally protected since the middle of 1995 (see also the section entitled 'Chilean Wine Law' on pages 62-63), when Chile conformed to the practice preferred in the international export market, that of defining smaller wine-growing areas for quality wines. Previously, things were not so strictly defined. Without question more Maipo (a subregion of the Central Valley) wine was sold in the past than the grapes in the valley were capable of producing.

With the exception of the Francisco de Aguirre vineyard in the Limarí Valley, there is hardly any production of wine left in the two northernmost regions of Atacama and Coquimbo. Whilst both are traditionally wine-producing areas, production has been switched over almost exclusively to table grapes and grapes for the manufacture of pisco.

Aconcagua

Of the principal wine-growing regions, Aconcagua is the northernmost and therefore the warmest. As a strong wind can blow in at the foot of the Aconcagua, the tallest mountain in the Americas, the vineyards are usually found in the side valleys which are protected from the wind. The main producer is Errázuriz, which is well-known for its Cabernets, the grapes for which are grown on calcareous soils.

Also belonging to the Aconcagua Region is the Casablanca Valley, which was only planted a few years ago. It contains a wide variety of soils, lies nearer to the sea, and every afternoon towards two o'clock it is cooled by Pacific winds, so that the harvest comes one month later than it does inland in the Santiago region. Casablanca is the discovery of the last decade. It was the Santa Carolina vineyard which

PAGES 56-57: The Carmen vineyards in Maipo Valley.
LEFT: The traditional vineyards near Panquehue lie in the Aconcagua Valley to the north of Santiago as does the Casablanca region which was only developed a few years ago.
MIDDLE: Errázuriz's bodegas also lie in the old Aconcagua Valley. In the last century one of the largest areas of vines under cultivation in private hands came into being here.
RIGHT: Many old vineyards can be found in the Maipo Valley, which thanks to its proximity to the capital can point to the most stable tradition of wine-growing over the course of the centuries.

did much pioneering work at the beginning, after the oenologist Pablo Morandé had made a first attempt to plant some vines there in 1982. From 1988, wines with a sophisticated structure began to appear, showing the great potential of the subregion. It was then that all of the larger Chilean companies and several foreign investors planted vineyards, although the valley is exposed to the dangers of a late frost. Vines currently under cultivation cover an area of approximately 1,900 ha (4,700 a), and the most prominent varieties are Chardonnay and Sauvignon Blanc. For the first time, Santa Carolina has succeeded in growing fruity red wine grapes in its Casablanca vineyard. A great future is predicted for the wines of the region, especially once the vineyards have reached the necessary age and the agronomists have gained more experience of the soils and microclimates to be found there.

Central Valley

This enormous region includes the Maipo, Rapel, Curicó and Maule subregions, all of which are a long way apart and have very different conditions for wine-growing.

Maipo, which is very close to Santiago, is the oldest wine-growing area in the Central Valley. The vineyards stretch from the foothills of the Andes along the Río Maipo valley towards the coast. For a long time, this location has been regarded as the best for wine in Chile. It has a low rainfall of 300 mm (12 in). Today, the main focus of the wine industry has changed, since firstly the city of Santiago has actually swallowed up a part of the older vineyards, and secondly cooler locations are preferred. Opinions are also divided as to whether the capital's smog is negatively affecting the microclimate.

Without doubt some of Chile's best red wines come from the Maipo Valley, which has predominantly alluvial soils as well as loamy ones, and gravel subsoils in several areas around rivers. Most of the vineyards which were founded more than 100 years ago are located here. Although there are approximately 4,800 ha (12,000 a) of vines under cultivation for wine production, there are also four times this amount of vines by area which are reserved for growing table grapes.

Further to the south, we find the Rapel Valley which has about 8,800 ha (22,000 a) of vines under cultivation for wine, and about the same amount for table grapes. Several rivers flow through this valley and with its very varied microclimates it produces interesting wines. For example, the San Carlos de Cunaco, Santa Mónica, Undurraga, Los Vascos, Torreón de Paredes and Viña Porta vineyards are located here, but at very different altitudes and on very different soils. Some of the most promising Cabernet Sauvignons in Chile come from here, and in particular from the Colchagua Valley.

The largest wine-growing area is located between Curicó and Talca.

Located here in the subregions Curicó and Maule are approximately 26,000 ha (64,000 a), or almost half of the land under cultivation for wine-making in Chile. Since the Central Valley is wider here and the flatness of the vineyards makes for easier work, wine-growing was able to spread very quickly. Quite a number of rivers flow through the area aside from the eponymous Maule, namely the Teno, Mataquito, Lontué, Claro and Lircay, all providing a source of water for irrigation. The climate is considerably more humid given that the annual rainfall is between 700 and 1,000 mm (28 and 40 in).

Wine-growers found sufficiently large areas for cultivation here with a proper summer heat. The soils range from the alluvial or the volcanic to being composed largely of sand or gravel, depending on how near they are to a river or mountain.

Southern Region

This region, which includes the Itata and Bío-Bío subregions and lies 400 km (250 mls) to the south of Santiago, does not enjoy a very high reputation. The main product of this area to date has been everyday wines in large amounts for the domestic market. There was at one time 27,000 ha (67,000 a) of large vineyards here, but in the past ten years half of these have been ripped out, since the largely traditional varieties, namely País and Moscatel de Alejandría were no longer required in such large amounts. The vines grew to a certain extent on almost boggy soils which provided a particularly high yield.

Interestingly, there are now occasional new plantings near Chillán, which show the region to have the potential for something different. The Southern Region is relatively cool and provided with sufficient rain (1,200-1,500 mm/47-59 in), and contains several areas influenced by volcanic activity which could be used for producing fresh, light white wines. The most spectacular new planting took place at the end of 1993 when the state-owned Itata SA planted 140 ha (345 a) of the four standard grape varieties, as well as Cabernet Franc and Syrah. Leading oenologists advise the company, which is currently building facilities worth in the region of almost £4.25 million (US$6.6 million). Itata has previously not bottled its own wines.

LEFT: In several vineyards the grapes are harvested in small wooden boxes and brought into the bodega.

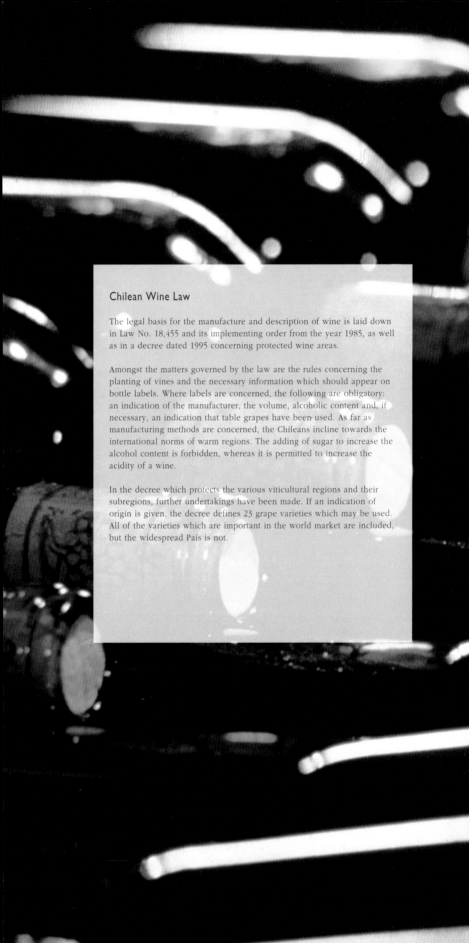

Chilean Wine Law

The legal basis for the manufacture and description of wine is laid down in Law No. 18,455 and its implementing order from the year 1985, as well as in a decree dated 1995 concerning protected wine areas.

Amongst the matters governed by the law are the rules concerning the planting of vines and the necessary information which should appear on bottle labels. Where labels are concerned, the following are obligatory: an indication of the manufacturer, the volume, alcoholic content and, if necessary, an indication that table grapes have been used. As far as manufacturing methods are concerned, the Chileans incline towards the international norms of warm regions. The adding of sugar to increase the alcohol content is forbidden, whereas it is permitted to increase the acidity of a wine.

In the decree which protects the various viticultural regions and their subregions, further undertakings have been made. If an indication of origin is given, the decree defines 23 grape varieties which may be used. All of the varieties which are important in the world market are included, but the widespread País is not.

A 75 per cent rule obtains where the vintage, exact origin and grape variety are concerned. This means that a wine can contain up to 25 per cent of other grape varieties, vintages and wine from other areas. Prior to the 1995 decree, the law covered only the disclosure of the grape variety, albeit on an 85 per cent basis.

The Chilean wine law prescribes that wines up to a maximum of 9 grams are called *seco* (dry), if there is a minimum of 7 grams acid present, and so forth, although there are practically no sweet wines.

Such terms as *Reserva, Gran Reserva, Reserva Especial* and the like are exclusively reserved for wines for which a place of origin is indicated. There is no rule, however, governing when such a wine can be called Reserva and so forth. There is an equal lack of legislation as to when a wine can be described as *vino fino* – as opposed to *vino corriente*, which is used for ordinary table wine which is usually slightly sweet. The former is normally used for all export wines.

In order to display the place of origin on a wine, bodegas must be a member of a commission which also supervises the observance of the regulations.

Exports of Bottled Wine from Chile 1995

Country	Amount (9 litre cases)	Value (US$ million)
USA	2,605,395	40.3
United Kingdom	1,308,879	24.3
Canada	665.522	12.6
Denmark	296,474	7.0
Holland	327,073	6.4
Ecuador	964,871	5.9
Sweden	243,656	5.2
Paraguay	407,530	5.4
Germany	171,289	4.3
Venezuela	232,249	4.1
Brazil	261,744	4,1
Columbia	214,316	3.9
Peru	315,014	3.7
Norway	129,498	3.5
Ireland	135,536	2.8
Other countries	1,226,795	20.8
Total	9,505,841	154.3

Source: Wine Export Association, Santiago 1996

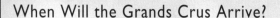

When Will the Grands Crus Arrive?

Ten years ago Chile was scarcely represented in the world wine market. When American journalists organized blind tastings with the first modern Chilean wines, they had to admit that Chilean Cabernets costing US$7 tasted better than Californian ones priced at US$15 and than many a Bordeaux one for US$20. It was then that the spell was broken.

In 1995, Chile exported approximately 129 million litres (34 million gal) of wine (of which two-thirds was bottled) and was the third largest importer into the United States of America. The wine industry contributed nearly US$182 million (£117.75 million) to Chilean exports in 1995. This growth in exports continues unabated.

Chile's strength lies in its ability to offer good wines competitively in the lower- to medium-price sectors. Blind tastings prove that Chilean wines are often better than considerably more expensive ones from other countries. However, the ambitious Chileans are not satisfied with an image of providing value for money. They want to have a say at the very top, and efforts are now being made in this direction. Vineyards such as Los Vascos, Carmen and the Mondavi/Errázuriz joint venture are already talking about their 'super wine', which will come on the market in two or three years time and is intended to line up alongside Latour, Gaja, Grange Hermitage or Vega Sicilia. A sense of expectation is quite justified. Just how quickly the development in quality is really happening was described very accurately by the American journalist Joshua Greene in 1995

when he observed that this is a revolution which is taking place in the vineyards. It was his opinion that only a few people in Chile two years previously were aware that very different wines could be grown in different locations, something which many even denied. In 1995, he observed that most Chileans in the wine industry were discussing this fact, which several wines had already proved.

The *terroir* is often still buried by large harvests or the effects of cellar technology. The low age of most valuable locations and high yields still work against the 'super wine' in many cases. The extraordinarily favourable conditions enjoyed by the Chileans for growing allow them to compete very easily with other countries despite their high yields. However, to produce wines of the highest concentration, for which brokers on the world market are prepared to pay over £8.50 (US$13.00) per bottle, the best vineyards have to be managed in an optimal way, and the grapes have to be processed in a similarly optimal fashion.

The separate development of different areas of wine cultivation, research into the best locations for specific grape varieties, the reduction of yields through economic irrigation, the selection of grapes and a further optimization in cellar technology are all fundamental steps which have already been taken along the way to the production of truly great Chilean wines. Several red wines (for example *Casa Real, Don Melchor*) and white wines (such as the Villard and Viña Porta Chardonnays) are today already scarcely inferior to the great, well-known competitors from California and France.

Pisco

Whether you make someone's acquaintance in Chile, are invited to someone's home or ask for a Chilean speciality in a restaurant, you will inevitably become acquainted with pisco. It is the Chilean national drink, although the Peruvians also produce their own pisco which is somewhat less strictly defined. It is drunk neat after a meal or as an aperitif in the very popular long drink Pisco Sour.

Chilean pisco is a true brandy like cognac, armagnac, German or Spanish brandy. It should not be confused with the many ordinary brandies which are consumed in South America in large quantities.

Brandies have been drunk in South America since the sixteenth century. However, pisco first appears in the year 1871, and there are several explanations for the name. Nicholas Faith believes that it is named after an Indian tribe called the Pisco, who made earthenware vessels in which the brandy was stored. Jan Read cites the Indian word *piscu* and the port of Pisco, from which the spirit was transported for years, as the origin of the name.

The government had already laid down strict rules in 1931 for the manufacture of pisco. These belong to the first rules of their kind governing the origin of brandy. Following a revised version of the law in 1985, pisco can only be made from grapes grown in the provinces of Atacama and Coquimbo. The grapes must be fermented into wine there, distilled into pisco and also matured there.

There are 13 grape varieties which are permitted in the production of pisco, of which today only five have any real commercial significance. They are Moscatel de Austria (2,376 ha/5,871 a), Pedro Jiménez (2,205 ha/5,449 a), Moscatel Rosada (2,051 ha/5,068 a) as well as the best grapes for making high-quality pisco, Moscatel de Alejandría (1,280 ha/3,163 a) and Torontel (884 ha/2,184 a). The amount of grapes under cultivation for pisco by surface area has been strongly on the increase since 1985 – from 5,875 to 9,087 ha (14,517 to 22,454 a). New plantings were in particular of the Moscatel Rosada and Moscatel de Alejandría grape varieties.

The most widespread grape variety is still Moscatel de Austria – a very neutral grape variety, but one which produces a large crop – taking up 26 per cent of the total area of vines under cultivation. Pedro Jiménez produces a similar yield, being a grape that grows well, contains a lot of alcohol and is neutral in flavour. It is very well suited to blending and accounts for 24 per cent of all pisco vines. The equally aromatic Torontel only produces good pisco when it is not planted in a vineyard which uses the all too productive pergola trellising, something which was often the case. Its share of vines under cultivation has contracted to just under 10 per cent.

Moscatel de Alejandría is both aromatic and characteristic, being the typical grape variety for the best piscos. The area planted with this variety has increased strongly, but still only represents about 14 per

The production of pisco is largely in the hands of the two co-operatives Control and Capel, whose technology is quite excellent.

cent of the total. Moscatel Rosada also produces excellent pisco, accounting for just under 23 per cent of vines by area.

In the distilleries the stems are removed from the grapes, which are then crushed. The skins are briefly steeped in the pulp to retain nuances of fruit and aroma. The temperature for fermentation, which previously stood at almost 30°C (86°F), at which a lot of flavour evaporated, is a thing of the past. Whilst it is true that the optimal temperature of 18°C (65°F) degrees is not used in the co-operatives, they do at least manage to remain below 25°C (77°F). After fermentation the wine contains about 12-14 per cent alcohol. It is distilled in tranches of 1,500 litres (400 gal) in wood-fired copper vats, like the ones used in the production of cognac. Distillation takes place up to between 50 and 60 per cent alcohol, although only the so-called 'heart' of the distillate is used. The beginning and end are added to the next batch of wine and distilled anew.

The distillate matures in barrels made from *raulí* (South American beech) or oak. If it were matured for a longer period of time the characteristic Muscat taste would disappear. For the purposes of marketing, the alcohol content is reduced through the addition of water to produce the four different types of pisco. *Selección*, the most straightforward type, is 30 per cent alcohol. This is followed by *Especial* at 35 per cent, *Reservado* at 40 per cent and *Gran Pisco* at 43 per cent. The longer the distillate remains in barrels, the higher is the resulting alcohol content and quality of the pisco. The Selecciones

Grapes for pisco come predominantly from the Elqui and Limarí Valleys, both several hundred kilometres north of Santiago. Here there is only one vineyard, Viña Francisco de Aguirre, which produces table wine.

are aromatic piscos with a taste of Muscat, whilst the stronger kinds which are more oaked, bear more of a resemblance to European brandy. At any rate pisco is colourless, as the barrels used scarcely impart any colour. Beyond the legally defined varieties there are also 46 per cent piscos, for which newer oak barriques are used, as well as pre-packaged Pisco Sour.

Two large co-operatives have almost 95 per cent of the market with the brands *Pisco Capel* and *Pisco Control*. There are also a handful of small brands such as *Pisco Casaux*, *Pisco Peralta* or the Valdivieso brand *Pisco Diaguitas*. Of all pisco produced, almost 90 per cent is drunk in Chile itself.

Pisco Sour

Whilst it is possible to buy Pisco Sour ready mixed, it is more elegant
to mix it yourself, which also produces a fresher drink. Take half a
bottle of pisco, one egg-white, the juice of one lemon (if necessary
half a lemon will do), enough crushed ice and sugar to taste. Mix all
the ingredients in a processor, to achieve a slightly creamy consistency. The drink is served in a glass which has been moistened briefly
and dipped in sugar, and a slice of lemon.

Vineyards and Wines

Large companies in many European wine-growing areas, focus on the production of popular wine of a rather unsophisticated quality. Most smaller companies in Chile would similarly be unable to compete in the aggressively priced market for everyday wines, which remains largely in the hands of the large enterprises. Nonetheless, these large Chilean producers are active also in the better quality wines, and a search for the ten best Chilean wines would certainly reveal five or six to be in their cellars.

As export is more profitable for Chilean producers than selling wine locally, the interest in important foreign markets is great. In 1995 the Chilean wine industry contributed approximately US$182 million (£117.75 million) to the country's exports. Only four companies handled rather more than half of all wine exported. These big four – Concha y Toro, Santa Rita, San Pedro and Santa Carolina – also dominate the domestic market.

This concentration in the industry proved to be advantageous during the crisis at the beginning of the 1980s, allowing an extraordinarily quick change of direction and modernization. The successive boom experienced in the last decade has produced a variety of new businesses, which have only been bottling for one or two vintages and which are still being built up.

The small, independent producer in the European tradition is absent in Chile, where a vineyard with an annual production of less than one million litres (265,000 gal) would actually be regarded as small. Concha y Toro, Santa Rita, San Pedro and Santa Carolina still remain indicative of the market with their policies on investment and brands. But even in the export market new vineyards have found market niches alongside medium-sized companies which are rich in tradition, such as Errázuriz, Undurraga or Cousiño Macul. Some were formed from what had previously been grape suppliers and manufacturers of wine from the cask (Carta Vieja, Viña Porta, Bisquertt, Santa Inés), who now took the opportunity to bottle their own wine. There were also instances of people investing from scratch in what they recognized to be Chile's enormous potential. Examples are the vineyards Discover Wine, Domaine Oriental, Tarapacá, Torreón de Paredes and TerraNoble.

Wine Regions, Valleys and Locations from North to South

Coquimbo	Elqui Valley	Vicuña
		Paiguano
	Limarí Valley	Ovalle
		Monte Patria
		Punitaqui
		Río Hurtado
	Choapa Valley	Salamanca
		Illapel
Aconcagua	Aconcagua Valley	Panquehue
	Casablanca Valley	
Central Valley	Maipo Valley	Santiago (Peñalolén, La Florida)
		Pirque
		Puente Alto
		Buin (Paine, San Bernardo)
		Isla de Maipo
		Talagante (Peñaflor, El Monte)
		Melipilla
	Rapel Valley	
	Cachapoal Valley	Rancagua (Graneros, Moztazal, Codegua, Olivar)
		Requinoa
		Rengo (Malloa, Quinta de Tilcoco)
		Peumo (Pichidegua, Las Cabras, San Vicente)
	Colchagua Valley	San Fernando
		Chimbarongo
		Nancagua (Placilla)
		Santa Cruz (Chepica)
		Palmilla
		Peralillo
	Curicó Valley	
	Teno Valley	Rauco (Hualañé)
		Romeral (Teno)
	Lontué Valley	Molina (Río Claro, Curicó)
		Sagrada Familia
	Maule Valley	
	Claro Valley	Talca (Maule, Pelarco)
		Pencahue
		San Clemente
	Loncomilla Valley	San Javier
		Villa Alegre
		Parral (Retiro)
		Linares (Yerbas Buenas)
	Tutuvén Valley	Cauquenes
Southern Region	Itata Valley	Chillán (Bulnes, San Carlos)
		Quillón (Ránquil, Florida)
		Portezuelo (Ninhue, Quirigüe, San Nicolás)
		Coelemu (Treguaco)
	Bío-Bío Valley	Yumbel (Laja)
		Mulchen (Nacimiento, Negreto)

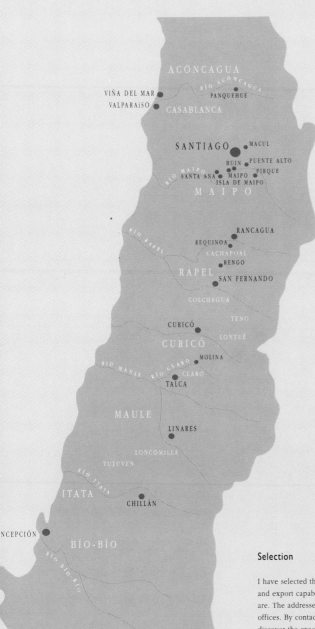

ACONCAGUA

RÍO ACONCAGUA

VIÑA DEL MAR
PANQUEHUE
VALPARAÍSO
CASABLANCA

SANTIAGO
MACUL

BUIN
PUENTE ALTO
SANTA ANA
PIRQUE
ISLA DE MAIPO
MAIPO

RÍO MAIPO

MAIPO

RANCAGUA
REQUINOA

RÍO RAPEL

CACHAPOAL
RENGO
RAPEL
SAN FERNANDO

COLCHAGUA

TENO

CURICÓ
LONTUÉ
CURICÓ

MOLINA

RÍO MAULE
RÍO CLARO
CLARO
TALCA

MAULE

LINARES

LONCOMILLA

TUTUVEN

RÍO ITATA

ITATA
CHILLÁN

NCEPCIÓN

BÍO-BÍO

RÍO BÍO-BÍO

Selection

I have selected the following bodegas according to size
and export capability as well as how well-known they
are. The addresses are as a rule those of representative
offices. By contacting them it will be possible to
discover the exact location of the wineries and to
arrange an actual visit.

Grading

Despite the need for caution, given that swift changes
in quality are always possible, I have elaborated a
system for grading the best wines (* for above average
wines, ** for Chilean wines of excellence, *** for world
class wines). The evaluation relates solely to the quality
of the specified wine, and not to the quality of the
vineyard, something which can vary a great deal at the
large houses.

Viña Aquitania

Av. Consistorial 5090 – Peñalolen, Casilla 213-12
La Reina – Santiago de Chile
TEL 2 – 2845470 | FAX 2 – 2845469

The three owners are Bruno Prats from Cos d'Estournel in Bordeaux, Paul Pontallier, the wine-maker from Château Margaux, and Felipe de Solminihac, who was regarded as the best oenologist in Chile in the year 1994. Their common goal is to strive for quality similar to the best wines of the New World. Pontallier and Prats decided to produce wine in Chile, following a one year visiting professorship by the Margaux oenologist. After a long search they found suitable soils of low fertility which were warm by day in the Maipo Valley, and in 1990 they planted about 25 ha (62 a) of Cabernet Sauvignon. The intention was that this would remain the only grape variety. The first wine, a 1993 vintage made from grapes which had been bought in, was bottled in 1994. The 1994 vintage became the first wine they had produced themselves. As far as irrigation is concerned, Solminihac takes his cue from the rainfalls in the best years for Bordeaux of all time. In the cellar he uses only a small amount of oak and allows the wines to macerate with the skins for two weeks after fermentation. The first wines show a mellow fruitiness combined with a somewhat more powerful tannin content.

Bruno Prats from Cos d'Estournel in Bordeaux, Paul Pontallier, the wine-maker from Château Margaux and Felipe de Solminihac, who was voted the 'best oenologist in Chile' in 1994, are a strong team. They founded Viña Aquitania in 1990.

Viña Balduzzi

Av. Balmaceda 1189
San Javier
TEL 73 – 322138 | FAX 73 – 322416

Jorge Balduzzi runs one of the smallest wine bottling businesses in Chile. With 30 ha (74 a) he scarcely produces more than 30,000 cases of wine a year, because he does not buy in any grapes. At San Javier near Linares he has bottled his wines since 1987, drawing on his vines which break down into 14 ha (35 a) of Sauvignon Blanc and 7 ha (17 a) each of Chardonnay and Cabernet Sauvignon. His cellar is equipped with *raulí* barrels as well as stainless steel tanks for controlled fermentation. The wines are well vinified. Particularly the Cabernet Sauvignon shows a pleasant mixture of oak and fruit aromas.

Viña Bisquertt

El Comendador 2264
Pedro de Valdivia Norte – Providencia – Santiago de Chile
TEL 2 – 2336681 | FAX 2 – 2319137

The Bisquertt family has been active in farming for five generations and in wine-growing for three. This distinguished family owns 400 ha (990 a) of vineyards near Lihueimo in the Colchagua Valley, several attractive country houses and a stud-farm. The old, very pretty winery on the road to Lihueimo was renovated and modernized several years ago. It is one of the few bodegas which has a stall selling its wine on the street.

Local conditions are more suited to growing red wines than white varieties, and as a result the larger part of the vineyard is planted with Cabernet Sauvignon and Merlot. Aside from these there are also some Chardonnay and Sauvignon Blanc vines. The family only bottles approximately one-quarter of each vintage, of which more than 90 per cent is sold abroad.

The house style in wines is still evolving. Hitherto, there have been several brands of average quality, including *Los Pedrones* and *Las Garzas*. The noticeably fruity reds, with their vegetal aromas and slightly bitter edge, sometimes taste as if they were harvested too early. A premium version of the *Doña Sol* brand made from selected grapes is planned.

The distinguished Bisquertt family produce their wines in an attractive, traditionally built winery in the Colchagua Valley under the *Los Pedrones* and *Las Garzas* brands.

Caliterra

Bandera 206, Oficina 601
Santiago de Chile
TEL 2 – 6994545 | FAX 2 – 6968572

Caliterra came into existence in 1989 as a partnership between the respected Chilean winery Errázuriz and the Californian Franciscan Vineyards. From 1992 the company has been entirely in the possession of the Chadwick family, who own the Errázuriz bodega. In 1995 Robert Mondavi took over 50 per cent of the share capital. Eduardo Chadwick is the president of both companies, which also co-operate in the spheres of production and marketing.

Since the takeover by the Chadwick family, Caliterra has planted its own vineyards in Casablanca (39 ha/96 a) and Maipo (40 ha/99 a). *Estate* wines were first produced from these locations in 1995. As was previously the case, the grapes for the more straightforward varietal wines (Chardonnay, Sauvignon Blanc, Cabernet Sauvignon) are bought in by Caliterra. There are long-term contracts for a total of 260 ha (643 a) in Casablanca, Maipo and Curicó. Annual production is in the region of 1.2 million litres of wine (320,000 gal), of which 85 per cent is exported.

For a long time the understanding was that Caliterra produced easily appreciated and somewhat better value versions of Errázuriz wines. However, the word is that a 'Super-Cabernet' of international standard will be produced in Maipo in the future. For several vintages Caliterra wines have had a very good international reputation for their cost: well-balanced, very typical Chardonnays (*) and Sauvignons, easy to appreciate, fruity red wines – whilst the Reserva reds have a fuller structure as they are matured in oak.

81

Viña Cánepa

Camino de lo Sierra 1500
Cerrillos – Santiago de Chile
TEL 2 – 5579121 | FAX 2 – 5579186

The large, modern functional building in Santiago-Cerrillos should not disguise the fact that Cánepa is still one of the family businesses in the Chilean wine-growing community, albeit one of the larger ones. The wine-maker Andrés Ilabaca has shown with the winery's most recent vintages that Cánepa can lay claim to a leading position amongst Chilean wine producers. José Cánepa founded the bodega in 1930, and today its vineyards cover 500 ha (1236 a) in three different locations in Rancagua, Sagrada Familia and Isla de Maipo. Cánepa produces quite large amounts of Sauvignon Blanc wines, as well as Chardonnay, Cabernet Sauvignon, Merlot and the more unusual Riesling, Pinot Noir, Malbec and Zinfandel.

Cánepa was amongst the first to draw conclusions from the crisis at the beginning of the 1980s, when it modernized its production facilities. In 1982 the family's was the first large winery to switch its production entirely to stainless steel and controlled fermentation. Today the winery has a capacity of 6.3 million litres (1.7 million gal) in stainless steel tanks and a further 1 million litres (264,000 gal) in large wooden barrels and barriques. Of a total production of almost 11 million litres (2.9 million gal), partly from grapes which have been bought in, a large part consists of straightforward domestic wines. Approximately 30 per cent is exported, above all to the United Kingdom.

Cánepa has acquitted itself very well over the last three years in many blind tastings with its premier wines. Its higher quality wines are sold under the Cánepa brand whilst further brands are *Hacienda St. George*, *Monte Nuevo* or *Peteroa*. Cánepa's quality wines begin with the straightforward *Sagrada Familia* range. There then follow the *Private Reserve* series. The top red wines *Finissimo* (*), Cabernet Sauvignon *Private Reserve* (**) and *Magnificum* (***) are mellow, harmonious wines which are very pleasant to drink and like the 1994 Chardonnay *Private Reserve* (***) belong to the best Chilean wines available. The velvety, concentrated Merlot *San Fernando* is excellent value given its quality. Unfortunately the wine-maker Andrés Ilabaca left Cánepa in 1996.

Viña Carmen

Hendaya 60, Oficina 202
Las Condes – Santiago de Chile
TEL 2 – 3315322 | FAX 2 – 3315324

Wine-maker Alvaro Espinoza from Carmen has already surpassed the sister enterprise with his white wines.

The prosperous industrialist, financier and passionate wine enthusiast Ricardo Claro, who since 1981 has also been the majority shareholder in Santa Rita, in 1988 acquired the brand Carmen, which is over 100 years old, in order to breathe new life into it. This gave rise to one of the most ambitious capital investment projects ever seen in the Chilean wine industry. Near Alto Jahuel in the Maipo Valley, not a stone's throw from Santa Rita, a large, brand-new winery containing the very latest equipment was built. Carmen has an annual production of 1.7 million litres (450,000 gal) of wine, but is already capable of processing 4.5 million litres (1.2 million gal).

At first Claro intended to concentrate on export wine varieties which represented good value, in the style of Californian wines. In fact Carmen was exclusively active in the export markets. However, once a hypermodern winery had been built and the oenologist Alvaro Espinoza had been engaged, the concept changed almost automatically. Espinoza, who had gained experience at Château Margaux and Moët & Chandon cultivates a regular exchange of ideas with the American business partner Fetzer. He planted Chardonnay, Cabernet

Ricardo Claro built the very modern, internationally oriented winery Carmen very close to Santa Rita, qualitatively anything other than a second Santa Rita wine.

Sauvignon and Sauvignon Blanc, grafting in part on to American vines as a precaution, should phylloxera actually reach Chile. He planted Syrah and Sangiovese vines as well, since he saw the valley as possessing all the necessary Mediterranean characteristics.

Since Espinoza created a Cabernet Sauvignon *Gold Reserve* which he was delighted with, on a vineyard 3.5 ha (8.7 a) in size which was not irrigated, he has been considering abolishing irrigation in general. He is fanatical about quality. The winery, which works in the modern tradition and in an international style has certainly specialized in varietal wines and Reservas. However, the quality of its wines certainly allows them to compete with the best wines of its associate company. Espinoza's Chardonnays, the varietal (**) which is reminiscent of fresh, ripe apple, and especially the Reserva (***, pear, melon, vanilla bouquet, perfectly integrated oak, very long – the equal of great Burgundies), have belonged since the 1994 vintage to Chile's best, as have the 1995 Merlot Reserve (***) and the excellent Cabernet Sauvignon *Gold Reserve* (***).

Carta Vieja

Francisco Antonio Encina 231
Villa Alegre de Loncomilla
TEL 73 – 381612 | FAX 73 – 381681

The Del Pedregal family has been growing wine in the Maule Valley since 1825 and is currently in its sixth generation. Up to 1985 they sold their grapes and wines to large producers. It was in that year that Don Alberto Del Pedregal decided to bottle a house brand by the name of *Carta Vieja*. Since own bottling began annual production has quickly risen to just under four million litres (1 million gal) of wine, which is almost exclusively sold abroad.

Presiding over 500 ha (1,236 a) of their own vines, divided approximately equally between white and red varieties, the vineyard no longer needs to purchase wine or grapes. Chardonnay, Cabernet Sauvignon, Merlot and Sauvignon Blanc roughly account for one quarter each of all vines grown. A large part of the vineyards, which are over a quarter of a century old, have good potential to produce wines which are full of character. Aside from straightforward Chardonnay and Cabernet Sauvignon matured in tanks, there are also good Reservas of both varieties with a rustic fruitiness which are barrique aged.

Viña Casablanca

Rodrigo de Araya 1431
Santiago de Chile
TEL 2 – 2382855 ı FAX 2 – 2380307

The parent company Santa Carolina caused some confusion when it gave this young winery its name. The reason for this is that it is literally identical with the cool Casablanca Region which was newly discovered at the beginning of the 1980s. It was in this region that nearly all of the major producers had purchased sites. In order to make the confusion complete, the Casablanca bodega also sells red wines from the Maipo Valley.

The Casablanca vineyard St. Isabel Estate is a pioneering one in this region and the only one to attempt to grow red wines despite the difficult conditions. By now it grows 166 ha (410 a) of vines, consisting of Merlot (10 ha/25 a) and Cabernet Sauvignon (3 ha/7.5 a), the largest part consisting of Chardonnay (125 ha/310 a) as well as a small amount of Gewürztraminer (6 ha/15 a).

A system of drip irrigation optimizes these modern vineyards. The oenologist Ignacio Recabarren has gained experience in Napa Valley, the Medoc and New Zealand. The most respected maker of white wines in Chile sees the development of Casablanca wines as a kind of life's work.

Particularly worthy of mention are his successful Chardonnays (**) which possess an exotic freshness with a delicate acidity, and following some crop failures two excellent Cabernet Sauvignons (**).

Casas del Toqui

Fundo Santa Anita de Totihue
Casilla 176 – Requinoa
TEL & FAX 72 – 551197

The newly founded bodega is marketing its first wines under the *Las Casas del Toqui* brand. The enterprise is a joint project between the French Médoc Château Larose-Trintaudon, the family of Juan Granella and AGF France under the leadership of Larose-Trintaudon. The Granella family contributed their 90 ha (220 a) of vines in the Cachapoal Valley near Rancagua, including 10 ha (25 a) of fifty year old Cabernet Sauvignon vines. The vineyard only processes its own grapes into wine. The Larose-Trintaudon team under the leadership of Franck Bijon and wine-maker Philippe Dardenne took over technical responsibility. At the end of 1995, the newly equipped winery bottled its first 700,000 bottles. These included 1995 unoaked varietal wines made from Cabernet Sauvignon, Semillon and Chardonnay as well as a barrique matured Chardonnay *Grande Reserve*. With their recognizable, pronounced personality they provide something of a glimpse of the ambitious claims of the founders. The Semillon could just as easily be a more everyday white Bordeaux, the Cabernet (*) is an accomplished and successful unoaked wine which is fruity in the modern sense as well as youthful. The Chardonnay *Grande Reserve* (**) offers competent international barrique standard wine at a relatively favourable price.

RIGHT: Vineyard Concha y Toro (see page 90).

The history of some of the brand names belonging to this famous house takes us back to the year 1718, when the ancestors of the company's founder received the title Marquès de Casa Concha from King Philip V of Spain. In 1883 the former lawyer and finance minister of Chile, Marquès Don Melchor de Concha y Toro founded the bodega and orientated his production to French vines. His wife Emiliana Subercaseaux brought a vineyard in Pirque to their marriage, which remains the basis of the enterprise's operations to this day. In 1923, Concha y Toro was turned into a public limited company and carried out pioneering work in the field of exports. The company expanded rapidly in the 1960s, and today, with the Guilisasti Tagle family as its principal shareholder, is by far the largest producer of wine in Chile with an annual output of 64 million litres (17 million gal) of wine (1994). However, as a house it has always remained innovative. Its extensive wine catalogue ranges from the most basic bag-in-box wine to Cabernet Sauvignon of an international standard. Concha y Toro is also Chile's largest exporter, and for several years has been one of the five largest wine importers to the USA. It also owns vineyards such as Tocornal and Santa Emiliana which have their own vineyards, the export brand *Viña Maipo* as well as the widespread domestic brands *Clos de Pirque*, *Subercaseaux* and *Cono Sur*.

The grapes for at least one-third of total wine production are grown on proprietal vineyards covering 2,100 ha (5,189 a) in almost all of the important regions, including Casablanca, Lontué, Maule and the

For many years Götz von Gersdorff has been responsible for the quality of Concha y Toro wines.

famous Puente Alto vineyard on the Maipo, one of the best locations in Chile. All wines are bottled in the Pirque winery, which is a popular destination for tourists. The German wine-maker Götz von Gersdorff has been responsible for technical quality for over thirty years. The brand *Casillero del Diablo* was introduced by him in 1965. This represented a new and modern way of making red wine, hitherto unknown in Chile, which emphasized fruitiness and avoided oxidization. Casillero, as well as *Marquès de Casa Concha*, is a quality range and is one of the few Chilean brands to be sold widely both at home and abroad. At the pinnacle of Concha's achievement we find a single wine: *Don Melchor* (***). This is certainly one of the best red wines in the whole of South America. It is a majestic, full-bodied Cabernet Sauvignon in the best Médoc style from the Puente Alto vineyard. Other exceptional wines in the full-bodied style from this producer are the Cabernet Sauvignon (**) and Chardonnay (**) varieties of the Marquès brand.

The Puente Alto vineyard is regarded as one of the best in the whole of Chile. It provides the grapes for *Don Melchor.*

Viña Cousiño Macul

Av. Quilin 7100
Santiago de Chile
TEL 2 – 2841011 | FAX 2 – 2841509

Every educated Chilean has heard of the Cousiño Macul estate. Its wines and attractive botanical gardens are famous. The old, architecturally attractive family vineyard Cousiño Macul is located in the Maipo Valley, virtually in Santiago, with a room for sampling the wine which is popular with tourists.

There have been vineyards on the family's land since Chile's colonial period. Pedro de Valdivia transferred the estate to his friend Don Juan Jufré in 1546, and chronicles report that vineyards were already planted there at this time. Since 1856 the estate, certainly one of the richest in tradition that Chile has, has belonged to the Cousiño family of industrialists, which has many different business interests. Amongst its possessions are mines, transport companies and a brewery. The Cousiños also founded Chile's leading daily newspaper *El Mercurio*.

Just under 300 ha (741 a) of vineyards, mainly growing Cabernet Sauvignon vines as well as Chardonnay, Sauvignon Blanc and Merlot are located around the vineyard in traditional, sound Maipo locations. Altogether the bodega has an annual harvest of about two million litres (530,000 gal) of quality wine. It has been a tradition since the last century to eschew the buying in of grapes or wine, just as it has been to avoid the production of unsophisticated wine for mass consumption. From a technical point of view the winery pursued for too long a very traditional course and at the beginning of the 1990s was overtaken by its competitors in the realm of quality. The owners have

Cousiño Macul is one of the vineyards of Chile most steeped in tradition. Located close to Santiago, it is frequented by many visitors.

modernized grape processing and fermentation technology in the last three years, investing substantial amounts of money. However, the goal is still to preserve the style of its typical red wines (Cabernet Sauvignon Reserva: *). These are peppery, full-flavoured wines with mature, mild tannins, and whose colour is not too dark. White wines produced from grapes grown in the warm hillside locations of the Maipo Valley lack something in finesse. A new red wine of excellence, the 1992 *Finis Terrae* (**), was launched in 1995, and the 1993 vintage (***) belongs amongst the best Chilean red wines.

Discover Wine

California 2521
Providencia – Santiago de Chile
TEL 2 – 2741703 | FAX 2 – 2250174

The Curicó Valley is home to this vineyard, which in many respects is an exemplary one. It is a classic example of the situation prevailing in Chilean wine-growing from the middle of the 1980s onwards. Once a series of dusty roads and hidden turnings have been negotiated, something wonderful awaits the inquisitive traveller. Not only the perfection which informs every aspect of wine-growing and production here is a source of wonder. The owners' country house, which is beautifully located on a bend in a river, is also well worth seeing.

Since the estate was founded in 1988, four people from the wine world have combined in exemplary fashion to create a winning team. Aurelio Montes, the gifted oenologist, leaves nothing at the winery to chance. He contributed vineyards and is in charge of wine production. Pedro Grand made a similarly valuable contribution with the Nogales vineyard (60 ha/148 a). Alfredo Vidaurre and Douglas Murray have gained decades of experience in marketing and exporting wines. These four prime movers have a good mutual understanding and a united vision of the direction of the enterprise. They bought an old winery, modernized it and today produce approximately 1.3 million litres (350,000 gal) of wine, of which just under one million litres (264,000 gal) is made from grapes from their vineyards covering over 100 ha (247 a). By 1997, this will have increased to 193 ha (477 a), and their own production will reach approximately 1.4 million litres (370,000 gal) on a yield of 9 tonnes per hectare (3.6 tons per acre).

Douglas Murray, Alfredo Vidaurre, Aurelio Montes (left) and Pedro Grand (top) founded Discover Wine and quickly took it to a leading position amongst Chile's wine producers.

The harvest is a relatively early one, and harvesting and fermentation are geared to preserving grape aromas, through gentle handling and low filtration. International acclaim came quickly for the young vineyard for its *Montes* and *Nogales* brands. The critics have been particularly convinced by the juicy, deeply fruity and mellow red wines which are of an excellent quality. The leading product is *Montes Alpha* (***), aged in French oak and made from Cabernet Sauvignon vines which are over eighty years old. This is certainly one of the best Chilean red wines. As well as Cabernet Sauvignon, Discover Wine makes various Sauvignon Blancs with and without barrique ageing, a powerful Chardonnay from American oak, a Chardonnay (*) which has a slighter bouquet with vanilla from French oak in the Mersault style, as well as two Merlots. Almost the entire output of the enterprise is exported, above all to England, Ireland and Holland.

Viña Echeverría

Asturias 171, Oficina 205
Las Condes – Santiago de Chile
TEL 2 – 2074327 | FAX 2 – 2074328

The Echeverría family has been active in agriculture and wine-growing in Chile for 250 years, and its grapes were sought after. Those which are grown in various vineyards planted with superior clones are regarded as excellent. Harvesting is done by hand in small plastic boxes.

Echeverría belongs to the traditional grape producers and wine-producers, who decided at the beginning of the 1990s to bottle their own wines. In 1992 Echeverría bottled the first of proprietary wines. In 1995, almost one million bottles left this well-kept and attractive vineyard.

Bodega and vineyards are located in the Maule Region, 200 km (125 mls) to the south of Santiago. Out of a total of 70 ha (175 a), one-half are planted with Cabernet Sauvignon, whilst the rest is divided between Sauvignon Blanc and Chardonnay. On the evidence of the first vintages, the quality is already very promising, even if it is a little individual and the wines are not vinified in a hypermodern way. Echeverría's best wines are a fine Sauvignon Blanc in the Bordeaux style, a successful Chardonnay Reserve (*) which is capable of maturing further and a smoky, dark fruited Cabernet Reserve (*).

Viña Luis Felipe Edwards

Av. Vitacura 4130
Santiago de Chile
TEL 2 – 2062383 | FAX 2 – 2087775

The agreeable Luis Felipe Edwards and his wife own one of the less well-known bodegas, which has gone over to bottling its own brands. The wines they produce should be followed with interest. They have 200 ha (490 a) of vineyards in the Colchagua Valley, which are between five and forty-five years old. Of these, 85 per cent are Cabernet Sauvignon vines, which thrive best here. For two decades Edwards produced grapes and wines for large producers. Since 1993, he has bottled his own brand *Luis Felipe Edwards*. He has gained the services of the first class oenologist Gilbert Rokvam (Château Lafite-Rothschild and Los Vascos) as an adviser.

His first vintages show a faultless technique in both vineyard and cellar, above all the 1994 Cabernet Sauvignon Reserva (**), and prove that the good reputation of the Colchagua Valley is justified. Wines of both varieties are powerful and benefit from thoroughly well-ripened grapes. Oak does not obtrude and therefore the wines are uncomplicated and easy to drink.

Errázuriz

Av. Nueva Tajamar 481, Torre Sur, Oficina 503
Providencia – Santiago de Chile
TEL 2 – 2036688 | FAX 2 – 2036690

In 1995 Errázuriz celebrated its 125th anniversary. The winery building in the Aconcagua Valley still dates from the last century.

This likeable vineyard, which despite its size has a family atmosphere, has an old winery building which is worth seeing from an architectural point of view. The well-kept vineyards, which are located picturesquely around the winery, are decorated with geraniums, roses and canna. In 1995 the president and owner Eduardo Chadwick-Errázuriz announced an excellent vintage which coincided with Errázuriz's 125th anniversary.

Errázuriz presides over 500 ha (1,235 a) of land, of which slightly more than 300 ha (740 a) produce grapes. These vineyards are divided between the Aconcagua Valley (120 ha/295 a), the cool Casablanca Region (38 ha/94 a) and the Curicó Valley (151 ha/373 a). Including its subsidiary company Caliterra, Errázuriz has an annual production of approximately 3.2 million litres (850,000 gal) which it predominantly ships abroad.

Errázuriz lies in the idyllic Aconcagua Valley, 200 km (125 mls) to the north of Santiago, and along with Villard, is the only vineyard there worthy of mention. Locations in the northern wine-growing region of Panquehue have an unusual preponderance of limestone soils for Chile, a Mediterranean climate and mild, cool Atlantic winds.

An ancestor of the present owner, Don Maximiano Errázuriz bought some land in 1870, and founded the vineyard. Having at that time

over 1,000 ha (2,500 a) of vines under cultivation, it represented the largest private estate in the world, and still remains in the family's possession. Errázuriz is one of the oldest bodegas in Chile as well as being one of the most respected. Wine-makers with international experience, who since 1994 have been under the direction of New Zealander Brian Bicknell, exclusively process Cabernet Sauvignon, Merlot, Chardonnay and Sauvignon Blanc grapes from proprietary vineyards.

The winery emphasizes that the blending of wines of different origins allows Chilean producers to combine several positive elements. Nonetheless, the best wines come from delimited areas. The house style is for refined wines which possess a playful elegance. Sauvignon Blanc and Chardonnay (*) from the Casablanca Valley and Merlot (*) from Maule are both equally in accord with this house style, as is the premier product from Errázuriz, the Cabernet Sauvignon *Don Maximiano* (**, Special Reserve ***), which comes from the eponymous vineyard near the winery, and which is matured in French oak for two years. It is an exemplary Chilean Cabernet with a fruity freshness and a bouquet of eucalyptus, which despite its refinement is powerful in body.

Viña William Fèvre

Huelen 56
Providencia – Santiago de Chile
TEL 2 – 2351919 | FAX 2 – 2354525

William Fèvre Chile was founded in 1991. Participants in the enterprise are William Fèvre, the respected producer of Chablis, and Victor Pino, who contributed estates. Fèvre Chile produces Chardonnays from the Arrigorriaga site in San Juan de Pirque and the La Parcela site, as well as a Cabernet Sauvignon from Miramonte de San Fernando. Fèvre is presently building a new winery in San Luis de Pirque. In San Luis experiments are taking place with various French clones, as well as with Pinot Noir and Merlot. Some of the wine is bottled in Chile, the rest being shipped to France after fermentation, before ageing in barriques begins. In France the wine is supervised by French wine-makers who make more Chablis Grand Cru for Fèvre than is made by any other producer.

The most important product of Fèvre Chile is the straightforward Chardonnay *San Juan*, which is bottled in France. Despite being 13 per cent alcohol by volume, this is an easy drinking wine from the vineyard which is 36 ha (89 a) in area and lies 750 m (2,500 ft) above sea level.

Viña La Fortuna

Camino a la Costa 901
Comuna Sagrada Familia, Casilla 19 – Lontué
TEL 75 – 471023 | FAX 75 – 471175

Daniel Güell Coll founded this enterprise in the Lontué Valley in 1943. Since then, the estate has been turned into a limited company, which remains in family hands. Out of a total of 2,500 ha (6,200 a) of fruit under cultivation, wines are only one of many sources of income. Of a total of 186 ha (460 a) of vines under cultivation, the principal vines are Cabernet Sauvignon (63 ha/155 a) and Semillon (27 ha/65 a), followed by Merlot (21 ha/50 a), Malbec (11 ha/27 a) and Chardonnay (10 ha/25 a). The bodega places its export capacity in the region of 800,000 litres (210,000 gal).

La Fortuna is one of the few Chilean bodegas to have Malbec (*) as a grape variety on offer, and its earthy fruitiness and slightly smoky emphasis makes it a good representative of the grape. A powerful Chardonnay Reserve (**) is the best wine from this producer. Cabernet Sauvignon with ripe and mellow tannins is another speciality. All wines show evidence of very competent cellar work.

Viña Francisco de Aguirre

Av. Nueva Los Leones 0145, Oficina C
Santiago de Chile
TEL 2 – 2321954 | FAX 2 – 3341517

This estate, which was laid out in 1992 by Pisco Control, is named after the man who founded the city of La Serena, and who also planted one of the first vineyards in Chile. The estate lies near Ovalle in the Limarí Valley, more northerly than every other bodega of note in Chile, a distance of 450 km (280 mls) from Santiago. It is the first wine estate in Region IV, where previously grapes have only been cultivated for the manufacture of pisco.

Following the planting of 60 ha (150 a) of vineyards in 1993, the first harvest could be brought in two years later. Grape varieties for everyday consumption of wine sold in Chile in litre cartons are Moscatel de Austria, Pedro Jiménez and Torontés. For the purposes of bottling and for export, modern grape varieties such as Cabernet Sauvignon, Cabernet Franc, Chardonnay, Sauvignon Blanc and an ungrafted Moscatel de Austria are grown. There are four different brands: *Doña Gabriela* and *Palo Alto* for tank fermented wines, *Piedras Altas* for wines matured in American and French oak and *Tierras Altas* for a Cabernet Sauvignon aged in French barriques.

Wines matured in tanks are characterized by an unusually flowery fruitiness. The Chardonnay and the Cabernet Franc *Palo Alto* (*) represent extraordinarily good value for money in particular. The premier brand *Piedras Altas* has immediately taken its place amongst the leading Chilean wines of the variety with an exotically elegant Chardonnay (**).

Casa Lapostolle/Domaine Rabat

Benjamín 2935, Oficina 801
Las Condes – Santiago de Chile
TEL 2 – 2429775 | FAX 2 – 2344536

Antonio Rabat was an ambitious young man. In 1902, at the age of sixteen, he left his home in Catalonia and embarked on a ship bound for South America. He came to Chile by crossing the Andes on the back of a mule. In 1920 he switched from baking to the wine business and in 1932 he purchased the Santa Adela de Manquehue Farm, to the east of Santiago. He planted French vines which he had brought with him from France on 150 ha (370 a) of the total available area of 500 ha (1,250 a). Once these former vineyards were turned into building land in the 1970s for a suburb of Santiago, the vineyard finally moved to Colchagua and Pirque in 1980. There are now 170 ha (420 a) of the four standard grape varieties under cultivation. On the domestic market, Viña Manquehue is one of the very best brands, producing table wine, quality wine, bag-in-box wine, drinks containing wine and ordinary sparkling wine. The estate became the subject of a joint venture between the drinks multinational Grand Marnier (through the Marnier family) and the Rabat family in 1992, and it now works wholly separately from Viña Manquehue. Alexandra Marnier-Lapostolle took over the management of the estate, and an investment of several million dollars was made in equipping the winery anew. It then proved possible to secure the services of the famous Pomerol oenologist Michel Rolland to supervise the cellar. Lapostolle bottled its first wines in 1994. Of a total production of approximately 1.3 million litres (345,000 gal), about 60 per cent is exported. Rabat wines are of a good quality, whilst under the Lapostolle brand we find a well-made barrique Chardonnay (*) *Cuvée Alexandre* (**), a Merlot *Cuvée Alexandre* (**) with a very sweet bouquet of French oak and a Cabernet Sauvignon which has a smoky concentration (**).

Viña La Rosa (Ossa)

Huérfanos 979, Oficina 819
Santiago de Chile
TEL 2 – 6332104 | FAX 2 – 6332106

This bodega, which has an attractive range of 1994 and 1995 wines, belongs to the Ossa family. It lies to the west of San Fernando in the Peumo Valley, and is one of the less well-known Chilean producers. Despite this, its wines are of a very good quality. Founded in 1824 by Gregorio Ossa, the estate was enlarged and modernized from 1930 onwards by Recaredo Ossa. There are 400 ha (990 a) of vines and on principle only the estate's own grapes are used in production. The microclimates and soils in different locations throughout the Peumo Valley and the smaller valleys of Cornellana and Palmería produce Cabernet Sauvignon, Merlot, Sauvignon Blanc and Chardonnay with widely varying characteristics.

The family business is run today by Recaredo Ossa Balmaceda, representing the sixth generation. He is advised by one of the best oenologists in the country, Ignacio Recabarren. Wines marketed under the *La Palma* brand not only have a pronounced flavour, but are the product of the technically faultless fermentation of a healthy grape harvest, ripened to perfection. The juicy, green Sauvignon Blanc (**), the buttery, mature Chardonnay (**) and the dense Merlot (*) are convincing varietal wines.

RIGHT: A rare combination. Palms and vineyards next to one another in the Palmería Valley, where La Rosa has planted some of its vineyards.

Vinos Los Robles

Coop. Vitivinícola de Curicó
Balmaceda 565 – Curicó
TEL 75 – 310047 | FAX 75 – 310345

Founded in 1939 by several wine-growers from the Curicó Region, the 500 members of the co-operative have an annual production of 10,000 tonnes (11,000 tons) of grapes and 7 million litres (1.85 million gal) of wine. The emphasis is on white wine, indeed, almost half of production is in Sauvignon Blanc. Cabernet Sauvignon, Semillon and Merlot are other important grape varieties. Some of the wines are still sold in barrels, whilst the larger part is sold under different brand names both at home and abroad. The most famous brand is *Los Robles*. The brand name *F.J. Correa Errázuriz* is an exclusive line which includes a very good Chardonnay (*).

Los Vascos

Benjamin 2944, Oficina 31
Las Condes – Santiago de Chile
TEL 2 – 2326633 | FAX 2 – 2314373

María Echenique and Jorge Eyzaguirre, the founders of Los Vascos.

This estate has one the highest profiles of Chile's vineyards. Its family history stretches back a long way. Basque ancestors of the founders Jorge Eyzaguirre and María Echenique came to Chile in the 18th century, with the Echeniques beginning wine-growing around 1750. Los Vascos ('the Basques') was only founded in 1975, when 2,300 ha (5,700 a) of family land were returned, in the wake of the demise of Allende. Most of today's 300 ha (740 a) of vineyards are located in the winery's own valley which is protected from the wind with a microclimate particularly suited to growing Cabernet Sauvignon.

In 1985, the famous English wine writer Hugh Johnson visited the vineyard and named it the 'Lafite of South America'. The Rothschild château actually took an investment in 1988, and today has 52 per cent of the share capital. Since 1990, this 'small Lafite' has had excellent sales of its splendid Cabernet Sauvignon (**) which is lightly oaked. The success of this excellent wine in a mellow, warm style, is attributable to the skilful ability to make full use of the strengths of Chilean wine-growing. The estate's white wines rather stand in the shadow of its reds. The problem here lies with a lack of structure, which can be traced back to the estate's locations being exposed to too much heat.

Whilst the team of oenologists, under the leadership of the experi-

enced Lafite helmsman Gilbert Rokvam, would like to present a
'Chilean red super wine', the French owners are still resisting. It
would appear that the full potential is not being developed, in order
to keep competition at arm's length from French products. The combination of technical perfection in the Bordeaux style of production
and the optimal climatic conditions are already showing excellent
results in experiments with a *Reserva de Familia* (***).

Viñedos del Maule

Avda. San Miguel 2631
Casilla 394 – Talca
TEL 71 – 242342 | FAX 71 – 242289

Founded as the Cooperativa Vitivinícola de Talca in the Maule Valley in 1944, this enterprise became a joint-stock company in 1995. The former co-operative which consists of over seventy small and medium-sized wine-growers presides over a total of 2,200 ha (5,436 a) of vineyards which are mostly planted with Cabernet Sauvignon, Merlot, Sauvignon Blanc, Semillon and Chardonnay. The annual production of 15 million litres (4 million gal) is mainly exported to Europe, the USA and Canada.

Apart from large amounts of wine from the cask, the company also sells bottled wine of a slightly higher quality under the brands *Gran Vino Exposisión* and *Conde del Maule*, including barrique matured Cabernet Sauvignon and Merlot (*).

Viña MontGras

Eliodoro Yáñez 2942
Providencia – Santiago de Chile
TEL 2 – 2336857 | FAX 2 – 2316560

In 1993 the brothers Hernán and Eduardo Gras founded the vineyard MontGras in the Peralillo Valley, together with Christián Hartwig. The vineyard, one hour's drive to the west of San Fernando in the Colchagua Valley, has 120 ha (300 a) of vines. An extremely modern winery was constructed, and in 1994 the first vintage with varietal wines of somewhat medium-quality made from the four standard varieties was marketed. The best wine is a mellow, easily appreciated Merlot (*). Following the first vintage a clear improvement is noticeable, particularly in the barrique aged Chardonnay (*).

Viña Domaine Oriental

Camino Palmira km 3,5
Casilla 864 – Talca
TEL 71 – 242506 | FAX 71 – 242091

At the heart of the Maule Valley lies the old vineyard of Domaine Oriental, which was founded during the last century by Rodolfo Donoso. In 1989 four wine enthusiasts of French origin took it over along with the accompanying beautiful country house built in the colonial style. They equipped the winery and planted new vineyards. There are now 120 ha (297 a) of the four standard grape varieties Cabernet Sauvignon (70 ha/173 a), Chardonnay, Merlot and Sauvignon Blanc on two different sites. Present annual production stands at around 500,000 bottles of wine which are exclusively for the export market. In Chile, the bodega produces wine from the cask.

The vineyard's fruity varietal wines have a slightly too prominent acidity for Chilean tastes. They are nevertheless representative of standard modern quality, even if there are ambitious plans for the future. The best white is a blended Semillon-Sauvignon (*), partly barrique aged, with fresh apple and melon fruit and a lingering taste. I also enjoyed the 1992 Cabernet Sauvignon *Clos de Centenaire* (*) which is still somewhat abrasive, although it is a wine that is intended to age. It is partly made from grapes grown on vines which are over 100 years old.

In the heart of the Maule Valley there lies Domaine Oriental's winery, which was founded in the last century by Rodolfo Donoso.

Viña Porta

Av. El Bosque Norte 0140, Oficina 23
Las Condes – Santiago de Chile
TEL 2 – 2332311 | FAX 2 – 2328677

Jorge Gutiérrez tells the curious that it was a difficult decision for his family to leave Catalonia in 1954. However, they then found the 'Piedmont of Chile', as they call the region near Requinoa where they live, 100 km (62 mls) to the south of Santiago in the Cachapoal Valley. The Gutiérrez-Porta family purchased approximately 190 ha (470 a) here in 1979. The family's first thought was of exporting fruit. However, they planted an area of 25 ha (62 a) with Cabernet Sauvignon vines and at first sold the grapes. They subsequently realized the great potential for Chilean wine-growing and in 1985 a winery came into existence for the sale of wine from the cask. The next step came in 1990. They set about creating their own bodega Viña Porta with relatively low vineyard yields, watering three times a year, a policy of greening the vineyards, protective harvesting technology and modern facilities for taking delivery of the grapes and fermentation. Their intention was to create a Chilean 'vineyard boutique'. In 1992 there began a two year co-operation agreement with the Californian vineyard Clos du Val.

The oenologist Yves Pouzet from Chablis, who has gained practical experience in California and Chile, brought much to the project. Today there are 100 ha (247 a) of vines on the site which is 730 m (2,400 ft) above sea-level, and besides 50 ha (124 a) of Cabernet Sauvignon vines there are also Cabernet Franc, Merlot, Sauvignon Blanc and Chardonnay. The first 10,000 cases left the vineyard in June 1993.

From the beginning Pouzet has created impressive wines. The powerful, concentrated and well-balanced Cabernet Sauvignon Reserva (***) and the consummate, buttery Chardonnay (**) of an international character already show much of the potential which is to be found in these vineyards and in the general expertise of the personnel. Viña Porta is one of the vineyards which is well worth noting in the search for quality.

Viña Portal del Alto

Camino El Arpa s/n, Alto Jahuel
Casilla 182 – Buin
TEL 2 – 8212059 | FAX 2 – 8213371

Alejandro Hernández is an agronomist, oenologist and professor of both of these subject areas at the Universidad Católica in Santiago. He has also made a name for himself as a commentator on wine. In 1970 he founded the Portal del Alto vineyard, which is devoted to producing quality wine for export. Since 1994 a small portion of its wines have been on sale in Chile.

The 100 ha (247 a) of vineyards, which have an annual harvest of approximately 600,000 litres (160,000 gal), are divided between four individual estates. In San Juan de Pirque grapes with an intense aroma which are harvested late grow in a vineyard 800 m (2,600 ft) above sea-level. The Cabernet Sauvignon vineyard in San Fernando in the Rapel Valley was planted in 1902, and covers 20 ha (49 a). In Buin, 35 km (22 mls) south of Santiago and near Santa Rita, there is another Cabernet vineyard containing grapes of a higher quality as well as the winery itself. The largest area of vines is in Retiro in the southern Maule Valley.

As well as Chardonnay, Sauvignon Blanc, Merlot and Cabernet Sauvignon, Hernández has also planted Pinot Noir as well as the Bordeaux varieties Cabernet Franc and Petit Verdot. With its popular white and red wines Portal del Alto is one of the serious smaller houses.

Viña San Carlos

Pintor Cicarelli 235
Santiago de Chile
TEL 2 – 5519864 | FAX 2 – 5511410

The San Carlos de Cunaco family estate is very conscious of the wine-growing traditions of the very attractive Colchagua Valley, being one of the oldest of its kind in Chile. Since the middle of the nineteenth century, French vines have thrived here in a sunny climate under the protective shield of the Andes.

In 1966, Miguel Viu Manent took over the vineyards and the cellar, which was over 100 years old. Up until 1990 he supplied large wineries, and since then he has been bottling his own brands *Viu Manent* and *San Carlos*. Aurelio Montes, one of the proprietors of Discover Wine, advises him on aspects of cellar technology.

The general impression is one of respectable medium-range quality wine. I most enjoyed a mature, well-balanced 1991 Cabernet Sauvignon.

The San Carlos de Cunaco estate has a total of 200 ha (494 a) of vines under cultivation, of which 150 ha (371 a) are to be found on the Hacienda San Carlos, where Cabernet Sauvignon, Malbec, Sauvignon Blanc, Chardonnay (*) and Semillon are grown.

The La Capilla vineyard, approximately 20 km (12 mls) away from the hacienda, has a further 50 ha (124 a) of Cabernet Sauvignon and Merlot. Wine-growing locations enjoy a favourable climate, with an annual rainfall of about 800 mm (32 in), strong daylight and considerable fluctuations in temperature between day and night. A network of canals and streams created by the Incas is used for irrigation.

Viña San Pedro

La Concepción 351
Providencia – Santiago de Chile
TEL 2 – 2352600 | FAX 2 – 2352411

San Pedro is one of the four giants in the Chilean wine world. Along with its subsidiary Santa Helena it has an annual production of over 30 million litres (7.9 million gal) of wine, of which 9 million litres (2.4 million gal) are exported. An impressive expanse of over 1,000 ha (2,500 a) of proprietary vineyards surrounds the winery near Molina. The company, which is steeped in tradition, was founded in 1865 and has in past decades been quite a pioneer. The French oenologist Pablo Pacotett Moinchot installed a refrigeration system as early as 1907 in the winery, something unparalleled in the rest of the world at that time.

Since 1980 majority control of the company has been held by a number of different investors. This has hindered any consistent reorganization and the installation of new production technology. Shortly after the takeover by the CCU Finance Group in the autumn of 1994, CCU began a US$25 million (£16.2 million) capital investment programme 'San Pedro 2000'. Advised by the French 'flying wine-maker' Jacques Lurton, San Pedro took the first step of bringing their white wine production right up to date. The results have been extraordinary. Even in the first year, despite having old facilities, San Pedro was able to produce fruity varietal white wines (Sauvignon/Semillon: *). Reasonably priced varietal wines with this degree of youthful clarity

With the new, enormous and hypermodern collection and fermentation station San Pedro succeeded in producing substantially better white wines from 1994 onwards.

are hard to find elsewhere in Chile. In 1995 a new fermentation station for white wine was built in the open countryside. Subsequent investments were made in the red wine sector.

The range of wines offered by San Pedro is very varied with several product lines on offer. This large winery plays an important role in the domestic market with a very high share of the market for everyday table wines in Tetrapak. The emphasis in exports is on brand and varietal wines which are competitive in price. The branded wine *Gato* (available in both white and red) is the most exported brand in Chile. Semillon and Riesling are offered alongside the standard varietal wines. The slightly oxidized *Las Encinas* (**) is the best-known white wine made along traditional lines in Chile and is one of several instances showing that this style is quite capable of producing interesting wines (available for export also as a red). Amongst the better quality wines in the prestige range *Castillo de Molina*, it is the rounded, oaked red wines (*) reminiscent of the Spanish tradition which have proved more convincing than the white.

Viña Santa Alicia

Camino Las Rosas s/n, Santa Rita
Pirque - Santiago de Chile
TEL 2 – 8546018 | FAX 2 – 8546010

This vineyard, which was founded in 1954, was previously known as
Viña Las Casas de Pirque. This was also the name given to several of
the brands it produced. Since 1993, under the Santa Alicia brand
name, everyday varietal wines have been produced, namely
Chardonnay, Merlot (which I preferred at tastings), Cabernet Sauvignon and Sauvignon Blanc, which is called 'Fumé Blanc' after the
American fashion. The same varieties are also bottled at reserve level.
Otherwise there are blended wines in the larger bottle size of 1.5
litres (54 fluid ounces).

Viña Santa Amalia

Camino Los Boldos s/n
Requinoa
TEL 72 – 551230 | FAX 72 – 551202

A holding company under the leadership of the French spirits company Massenez of Alsace purchased this vineyard in 1990. Santa Amalia,
which was first laid out in 1850, has 250 ha (618 a) of vines which
are on average 40 years old. The vines at Requinoa, about 80 km (50
mls) south of Santiago, are very close to the Andes on stony ground
and according to the producer are managed on an ecological basis.
The site has deep gravel soils which do not encourage a great deal of
growth and is particularly suitable for Cabernet Sauvignon, which
accounts for two-thirds of a total production of 1 million litres

Old oak barrels at Los Boldos. The Massenez family, who hail from the Alsace, took over the old winery in 1990.

(264,000 gal). Sauvignon Blanc and a small amount of Chardonnay, which is the only wine matured to oak, complete the range of vines. It was intended that the French oenologist Yves Pouzet, formerly active with William Fèvre in Chablis, would produce wines comparable with the high-quality spirits of Massenez. The examples I have tasted from the 1993 and 1994 vintages did not do justice to such aspirations, since much remains to be done in the winery and vineyards. The 1995 and 1996 red wines however do show progress. Wines bottled under the *Chateau Los Boldos* and *Santa Amalia* brands are sold exclusively abroad.

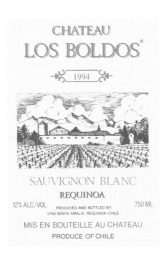

Viña Santa Carolina

Rodrigo de Araya 1431
Santiago de Chile
TEL 2 – 2382855 | FAX 2 –2380307

Founded by Luis Pereira in 1875, Santa Carolina has an annual production of 25 million litres (6.6 million gal). It is one of Chile's four
large wine producers and has wineries and subsidiaries in several
important wine-producing regions. As was the case with several vineyards which were newly planted in the nineteenth century, the history of Santa Carolina began with the importation of a French oenologist and a French master builder. The building which contains the
winery was built in 1875, and is now in Santiago. It is the company's
headquarters and there is a preservation order on it. Until the middle
of this century it was surrounded by the family's own vineyards,
which have since been sacrificed to the growth of the city.

Today Santa Carolina possesses vineyards and three further wineries
in Casablanca, Santa Rosa del Peral and Molina near Curicó. From its
own vineyards of 809 ha (2,000 a) and additional grapes which are
bought in, the vineyard produces everyday table wines, varietal
wines and high-quality Reserva and Gran Reserva wines, partly from
individual sites. Since 1989 the proportion of everyday wines produced for the domestic market has been almost halved and now only
accounts for 50 per cent of production, whilst the proportion of better wines has been doubled. 40 per cent of output and 60 per cent of
turnover is accounted for by export business, which is predominantly
carried out with the USA, Canada, United Kingdom and Ecuador.

Santa Carolina has taken over a leading role nationwide particularly
in the making of white wine. The oenologist Ignacio Recabarren has
gained a lot of experience at home and abroad and is regarded as the
leading authority on wine in Chile. Barrique fermented Reserva white
wines such as the Chardonnay (**) and Sauvignon Blanc (*Santa Rosa*:
***) are regularly counted amongst the finest Chilean wines. However,

The oenologists Ignacio Recabarren (top) and Pilar González have led Santa
Carolina away from being purely a volume producer. A range of top wines are
proof of this.

he pays particular attention to fruity white wines with a delicate acidity. He has been particularly enthusiastic about the cool Casablanca
region in recent years. He has laid out Chardonnay, Cabernet and
Sauvignon Blanc vineyards there for Santa Carolina and founded his
own Casablanca vineyard, which he runs. Pilar González is now in
charge of the parent company's wines.
Santa Carolina also knows how to produce red wines. The company's
powerful and well-structured Cabernet Sauvignon Reserva (*) and an
excellent 1990 Cabernet Sauvignon Gran Reserva (**) belong amongst
Chile's finest. Ochagavía, a vineyard which is over 100 years old, is
also a subsidiary of Santa Carolina today. Its Cabernet Sauvignon
Reserva (**) is very good and is somewhat more traditional and mellower than the Santa Carolina Reservas, which are rather fruity in the
international style.

Viña Santa Emiliana

Virginia Subercasaux 210
Pirque – Santiago de Chile
TEL 2 – 2202120 | FAX 2 – 2294459

1,672 ha (4,132 a) of land make Santa Emiliana one of the largest agricultural businesses in Chile. Over 1,000 ha (2,500 a) are already planted with vines. Nine different estates, in various locations including Rancagua, San Fernando, Rapel and Casablanca produce above all Cabernet Sauvignon, Merlot, Chardonnay and Sauvignon Blanc as well as Pinot Noir, Riesling and Gewürztraminer. Santa Emiliana also has contracts with wine-growers who regularly deliver grapes, and further purchases of wine cover its current annual requirements of about 7.5 million litres (1.98 million gal) of wine.

Santa Emiliana was founded in 1986 as a subsidiary of the Concha y Toro Group, but has since then come to be managed separately. It concentrates in particular on producing young, easy to drink, varietal wines for export, which have not been barrel matured and which represent good value for money. Brands are *Andes' Peaks* for everyday wines and the somewhat more sophisticated *Santa Emiliana*. The company is very successful in the USA with the *Walnut Crest* brand name.

Viña Santa Helena

Av. Vicuña Mackena 3600
Santiago de Chile
TEL 2 – 2382131 | FAX 2 – 2381747

Santa Helena came into being in 1930 as a brand of the Vinos de Chile bodega. In 1976 the San Pedro Group took over Santa Helena. In the future the subsidiary can expect to be granted more independence within the group.

As well as wine from the cask the estate produces everyday wines under the somewhat confusing brand name *Gran Vino* (Great Wine) and the varietal line *Siglo de Oro*. The prestige range selection *Selección del Directorio* is barrique aged with a rounded, easily appreciated Cabernet Sauvignon (*) and a Sauvignon Blanc which is presently still rather old-fashioned.

Viña Santa Inés

Manuel Rodriguez 229, Casilla 47
Isla de Maipo – Santiago
TEL 2 – 8192959 | FAX 2 – 8192986

The Italian Pietro de Martino settled 60 years ago in the Maipo Valley in Isla de Maipo, which retains its rural beauty today. He then began to produce wines with his brother Licino.

In due course the area of vines under cultivation has grown to 120 ha (297 a). The mainstay consists of Cabernet Sauvignon vines, and there are also Sauvignon Blanc, Chardonnay and Merlot. The winery, which was built in the 1960s, has very modern equipment. Five years ago Licino de Martino's grandsons began to bottle some of their own wines under the standard brand of *Santa Inés* and the prestige brand of *De Martino*.

Several of the wines, particularly the more ordinary ones, seemed overtreated to me. A good impression was made by the 1994 barrique fermented Chardonnay (*) in the De Martino range, a 1988 Cabernet Sauvignon unfiltered (*) with a particularly convincing bouquet and a fine 1990 Cabernet Sauvignon under the De Martino label.

Viña Santa Mónica

Camino a Doñihue km 5
Casilla 253 – Rancagua
TEL 72 – 231444 | FAX 72 – 225167

In 1976 Don Emilio de Solminihac, who owns the enterprise to this day, took over an old winery and 93 ha (230 a) of vineyards and founded Santa Mónica.

The winery, which is located about 90 km (56 mls) to the south of Santiago near Rancagua, and several of the vineyards have been in existence for several decades. One part of the vineyards which cover 93 ha (230 a) are even 65 years old. In 1976 Don Emilio de Solminihac took over the site and founded Santa Mónica, and he is still the owner today. An old country house which went with the property is presently being renovated, and plans are for it to be the company's representative office in the future. Proprietary vineyards produce half of the annual output of 2.5 million litres (660,000 gal). A part of the wine produced leaves the cellars in casks. About 75 per cent of bottled wine (50,000 cases) is exported.

Santa Mónica has largely remained a winery in the traditional style. However, Solminihac has modernized it to the extent that export wines can now be developed. Some of its wines are produced using traditional cooling and fermentation methods – some fermentation takes place in large wooden tanks. On the other hand, barrel fermented Chardonnay (*, with a banana bouquet, oily and heavy in character) is aged in 200 barriques made of French oak. The Cabernet Sauvignon (clean cherry bouquet) of the prestige range *Tierra del Sol* receives the same treatment, its grapes coming from old vineyards. Of these two wines Solminihac says that they are his vision of a great wine, possessing the elegance and cultivation of the Old World and a Chilean heart. As well as the standard grape varieties Santa Mónica also bottles smaller amounts of Semillon and Riesling.

Viña Santa Rita

Hendaya 60, Oficina 202
Santiago de Chile
TEL 2 – 3315222 | FAX 2 – 3315159

This producer, which is rich in tradition, has a tremendous presence in the market. With an annual production of 36 million litres (9.5 million gal), 6.5 million litres (1.7 million gal) of wine exported and over 1,000 ha (2,500 a) of its own vineyards, Santa Rita (including its sister company Viña Carmen with 1.7 million litres (449,000 gal) is the second largest wine company in Chile.

However, it is not only the enormous amount that it produces which makes this unusual house so fascinating. Its philosophy is one of quality and it is impressive to see how it implements this, whether it is a question of the most ordinary wines for the domestic market, keenly priced export items or high-quality luxury lines. The high-quality lines are not merely there as window dressing, but form an important part of sales policy. 8,000 oak barriques are evidence of the high proportion of barrel matured wines. No other bodega can lay claim to so many barriques.

Domingo Fernández Concha founded Santa Rita in 1880 on a site near Buin in the Maipo, where vineyards had previously stood a century before. The cellars, which were built at that time, are amongst the oldest which are still in use in Chile. As well as the well-tended winery in Buin with its extensive vineyards Santa Rita also owns vineyards in Rapel, Maule and Casablanca as well as sites in the Curicó Valley (Lontué) and a winery for the local market in Lirios. In recent years proprietary vines under cultivation have been more than doubled in size and trellising has been employed throughout. The plan is that by 1998 they will reach 1,300 ha (3,212 a) once further sites have been established in Casablanca. In contrast vineyard yields have been brought down. The company states that its Cabernet Sauvignon yield is between 6 and 7 tonnes per ha (2.4 and 2.8 tons per acre).

Fermentation and cellar technology was modernized to international

Cecilia Torres (above) and Andrés Ilabaca have been responsible for the quality of Santa Rita's wines since 1996.

standard in 1986. Santa Rita's longstanding oenologist Klaus Schröder has recently left and responsibility has passed to Cecilia Torres and Andrés Ilabaca (from Cánepa) since 1996. The everyday varietal wines are good, but the better wines profit from being oaked and a higher degree of concentration. The *120* range accounting for just under three-quarters of quality wine production forms the basis, and there then follow the *Reserva* and *Medalla Real* product lines. The top product *Casa Real*, an excellent Cabernet Sauvignon (***) is only produced in small amounts of 25,000 litres (6,600 gal), although not in bad years such as 1992. The top Cabernets – also *Medalla Real* (***) – regularly perform excellently in tastings at home and abroad and number amongst the best Chilean red wines year in year out. The concern's strength lay for a long time in red wines. The last three vintages have also produced interesting, well-structured and not too buttery Chardonnays (*Medalla Real*: **) which I have tasted. The quality of the 1994 *120* (*) was sensational for its price bracket. The Sauvignon Blanc has yet to achieve a similar breakthrough.

Viña Segú Ollé

Yumbel 383
Casilla 72 – Linares
TEL 73 – 210078 | FAX 73 – 214607

This company was founded in 1924 by Catalans. Its offices are in Linares and it presides over about 180 ha (445 a) of vineyards in San José de Caliboro in the Melozal Valley (Maule). The vineyards are watered from the Río Loncomilla and the climate is one of rather cool summer nights and cold winters. The Cabernet Sauvignon, Merlot, Semillon (80 ha/198 a), Riesling, Gewürztraminer, Sauvignon Blanc, Chardonnay, Moscatel and País vines were set out in the old way using low trellises, which results in lower vineyard yields than the widespread pergola system. Nonetheless, annual production in 1994 was in excess of 2 million litres (530,000 gal) – wholly from proprietary vines. The bodega calculates a yield of about 8,000 litres (2,100 gal) per ha for its Cabernet Sauvignon and 10,000 litres (2,640 gal) per ha for its Chardonnay.

Segú Ollé's wines have been exported since 1993. Its catalogue contains everyday blended and varietal wines, and in the latter case there is a Moscatel de Alejandría as well as the standard varieties. It also produces barrique aged Reservas and two sparkling wines which are fermented in tanks and are more or less sweet. Brand names are *Doña Consuelo* or *Caliboro.* The best – a Merlot – comes from the red clay soils around Linares.

Viña Tarapacá ex Zavala

Los Conquistatores 1700, Piso 16
Providencia – Santiago de Chile
TEL 2 – 2336611 | FAX 2 –2333162

Francisco de Rojas y Salamanca founded this vineyard in 1874 as Viña de Rojas and was soon planting French vine varieties at the foot of the Andes – Viña Tarapacá is therefore one of the oldest bodegas in Chile. Throughout its long life the enterprise has had a series of owners. Fosforos Holding acquired it in 1992 and invested £19.4 million (US$30 million) in cellar technology and in buying 2,600 ha (6,425 a) of land – a whole basin-shaped valley near Rosarío de Naltahua in

Tarapacá is one of Chile's oldest wineries. The Cabernet Gran Reserva matures for a very long time in oak barrels.

the Maipo Valley. Between 1992 and 1995 430 ha (1,065 a) of vines were planted.

In addition there is the traditional vineyard Tobalaba to the east of Santiago which has 70 ha (173 a) of vines, which are 40 years old and of a high quality. Cabernet Sauvignon accounts for most of the vines, and there are also Merlot and Chardonnay. Total annual production is reckoned at 12 tonnes per hectare (4.8 tons per acre) in the newer vineyards and at just under one million litres (264,000 gal) of wine, of which a growing proportion (1994: 35 per cent) is exported. The future goal is for an annual production of four million litres (1.1 million gal) of wine. The cellars of the bodega near Rosario are new and have modern equipment. American and French oak barrels are used for maturing. The first wines from the new winery were produced in 1996, and so we must await developments.

The export range consists of six wines. These are varietal wines of medium quality (Cabernet Sauvignon and Chardonnay), the premium *Gran Tarapacá* as well as a modest Chardonnay, a very good, juicy Merlot (*) and finally an impressive Cabernet Sauvignon Gran Reserva (*, full-flavoured toasted bouquet from lengthy oak maturation, with a lingering flavour) as its prestige wine.

Viñedos TerraNoble

Av. Andrès Bello 2777, Oficina 901
Las Condes – Santiago de Chile
TEL 2 – 2033360 | FAX 2 – 2033361

Six shareholders, including the French oenologist Henri Marionnet
began TerraNoble in 1992 by investing £1.6 million (US$2.5 million).
They built a winery in San Clemente in the Maule Valley, planted 90
ha (222 a) anew and purchased 30 ha (74 a) of existing vines. The
vine varieties under cultivation are Merlot and Sauvignon Blanc.

It is Marionnet's belief that Chile will be one of the most important
wine-growing countries of the 21st century. He brought Sauvignon
vines with him from his home in the Loire Valley, whose grapes are
fermented without cultured yeast to preserve their own aromas as
happens with Merlot. Hand picking, whole bunch pressing and the
avoidance of any contact with air are just as much a part of the philosophy of the winery as are strict temperature control both during
and after bottling as well as extreme hygiene in the cellars.

TerraNoble brought its first wines on to the market in the autumn of
1994: a Sauvignon Blanc and Merlot of the 1994 vintage. The vineyard concentrates on Merlot, which was already under cultivation in
the cooler climate of the Talca Region to the south of Santiago. It is
vinified using the technique of carbonic maceration and was praised,
in my view slightly excessively, by the American journal *Wine &
Spirits*, as quite an exciting wine with a considerable raspberry bouquet. The Sauvignon (**), made in a fresh Sancerre style, has really
been very successful and has received much critical acclaim.

Viñedos Torreón de Paredes

Av. Apoquindo 5500
Las Condes – Santiago de Chile
TEL 2 – 2115323 | FAX 2 – 2462684

Amando Paredes, a successful entrepreneur from the world of metal processing, founded the Torreón de Paredes vineyard in 1979 at the age of 70. He bought an attractive old country house built in the colonial style in Rengo, to the south of the Río Cachapoal, which came with a small vineyard. Vines under cultivation have since swelled to 150 ha (371 a). The vines are expected to work hard in the extremely stony soils, so that good grapes grow. It is the opinion of Amando's two sons Javier and Alvaro that the vineyards are the cornerstone of the estate's approach to quality. Both gave up their previous careers to help on the family estate. Torreón de Paredes works exclusively with its own grapes and sells only its own wine. 4,000 vines planted closely together, a low level of fertilization, drip irrigation and low yields of no more than 9 tonnes per hectare (3.6 tons per acre) really are good preconditions for creating quality. Optimal conditions are achieved in the cellars by the use of the most modern stainless steel technology and new French oak barrels should further improve cellar conditions in the near future. All wines are fermented with French dried yeast. Since the 1995 vintage the oenologist Ernesto Jinsan who had previously worked for Errázuriz joined the estate to establish standards of quality.

The Paredes place great emphasis on Cabernet Sauvignon, which in their opinion flourishes very well in the alluvial soils at Rengo in the Rapel Valley. For the Cabernet Reserve, aged for 10-14 months in French barriques, they are striving to produce rich fruit flavours of ripe cherries, blackberries, eucalyptus and tobacco, mild tannins and a silky texture. The tannins in the 1987 *Colección Privada* precluded that wine from achieving such an ambition. A 1994 Merlot Reserva (*) and a 1995 Cabernet Sauvignon Reserva (**) in the style of a rather traditional Spanish red wine do however show a clear house character. The Paredes also produce an oaked Sauvignon Blanc (*, clear gooseberry, very clean, easily appreciated, and at 13.5 per cent alcohol quite strong), a Merlot produced in stainless steel tanks and two Chardonnays: a fruity one from the stainless steel tank and an oak fermented one with a long fermentation period.

PAGE 130: At the age of 70, Amando Paredes, a successful industrialist in the metal processing sector founded the Torreón de Paredes vineyard in 1979.

Miguel Torres

Panamericana Sur km 195
Curicó
TEL 75 – 310455 | FAX 75 – 312355

Miguel Torres, the pioneer of growing quality wine in Spain, today remains a model for many Spanish wine-makers with new grape varieties, his own vine cultivation and modern cellar technology. When he founded his bodega in Chile in 1979 he was also an original, because he was the first to equip his winery with stainless steel technology and fermentation tanks which could be cooled.

To the original plot of about 100 ha (250 a) of land in Curicó were added 53 ha (131 a) in Lontué in 1986 and 72 ha (178 a) in Río Claro in 1990. As well as the four standard varieties less Merlot, the vineyard produces some Riesling, Gewürztraminer and Pinot Noir. Annual production is at around 750,000 litres (200,000 gal), 75 per cent of which is exported. Unlike in Spain, Torres is no longer at the absolute forefront of wine-making in Chile, although he supervises the Chilean harvest personally every year. Except for a very good Cabernet Sauvignon *Manso de Velasco* (*, a slightly toasted flavour, medium body) and an interesting sparkling wine in a fresh, fruity style, the estate's output is of wines of an average quality.

Viña Undurraga

Lota 2305
Providencia – Santiago de Chile
TEL 2 – 2326687 | FAX 2 – 2341676

Undurraga describes itself as 'la mejor familia de vinos' (the best family for wine) in the brochure for its products, thus leaving the question open as to whether the superlative refers more to the family business or to the quality of the wine. Particularly in the export sphere Undurraga has without question carried out pioneering work. At least with its unmistakable bottles Undurraga still maintains a special position today. The well-kept old bodega is also worth seeing with its cellar full of wooden barrels and its park like surroundings near Santa Ana in the Maipo Valley.

Like many Chilean wineries, Undurraga was also founded in the 1880s. Francisco Undurraga – like his descendants – laid particular emphasis on the wood used for his barrels. Large oak barrels of Bosnian and American oak still give the red wines their character today. Presently, the fermentation technology is being modernized and from the 1997 harvest onwards will be the equal of standards prevailing internationally.

The old bodega in the Maipo Valley consisted of 120 ha (297 a), to which a further 200 ha (494 a) have been added in the Colchagua Region near Palmilla. About 45 per cent of an annual output of 5 million litres (1.3 million gal) is exported.

The Undurraga family has run the enterprise for five generations, although it has now been turned into a limited company. It would appear that the new management associated with this has also had a beneficial effect on quality, as for a while Undurraga wines were at best of an average standard. As well as the normal vine varieties to be found in Chile, Undurraga has specialized in Pinot Noir, which rarely possesses the cherry fruit so typical of the variety, although it should be stressed that this is the case elsewhere in Chile as well. Another house speciality is a Riesling which has been barrel matured for two years. The fresh Sauvignon Blanc is also proving very suc-

The well-tended old bodega of Undurraga near Santa Ana in the Maipo Valley is well worth seeing, with its cellars full of wooden barrels and its surrounding park.

cessful at present. Prestige ranges are the *Viejo-Roble* wines which are exposed to wood for two years and the *Bodega de Familia* range which has a very good Cabernet Sauvignon (*) in the traditional style.

Viña Valdivieso

Juan Mitjans 200
Santiago de Chile
TEL 2 – 2382511 | FAX 2 – 2382383

When Alberto Valdivieso fermented his first sparkling wines, his intention was that they should be like champagne, as good as the fine Cliquot which had brightened up his student days in Paris. He travelled the Champagne region, brought a French wine-maker to Chile, planted Chardonnay and Pinot Noir, versed himself in classic bottle fermentation and in 1887 opened the first bottle of his own making. Soon his 'Chilean champagne' belonged in every prosperous household.

Shortly after the turn of the century Valdivieso also began to produce still wine. This wine enjoyed such a high reputation that the respect in which a person was held was measured by whether they were offered it. Today a part of the grapes for still wine production are grown on 150 ha (371 a) of proprietary vineyards in the Lontué Valley and the Maipo Valley. In contrast to the sparkling wines, Valdivieso's still wine is almost exclusively exported, with 70 per cent going to the USA under the successful *Morillon* brand. Since 1949 Valdivieso has belonged to the Mitjans Group, which was founded by Juan Mitjans over 70 years ago as a wine business.

Today the family enterprise specializes in spirits and has three-quarters of the Chilean market. Amongst its products are the pisco brand

Sparkling wine still accounts for three-quarters of the concern's total production of 3.6 million litres (950,000 gal).

Diaguitas, Tres Palo brandy, many liqueurs and imported spirits.

The old and architecturally attractive winery has several floors in its cellar for bottle fermentation, of which some are still in use today. The building and cellar technology were brought up to the highest technical standard a few years ago. Three-quarters of today's annual production of 3.6 million litres (950,000 gal) still consists of sparkling wine – four out of five bottles of Chilean sparkling wine carry a Valdivieso label. The best is without question the buttery and mellow *Valdivieso extra brut* (**, Chardonnay/Pinot Noir), which is made with classic bottle fermentation techniques. As well as the normal varietal wines, Valdivieso produces good Cabernets (*, the 1993 with its fresh and refined acidity was reminiscent of wines from Tuscany), Merlots and Chardonnays (**) aged in barriques. The buttery Chardonnay with an exotic fruit bouquet could just as well come from California if it were more expensive.

Villard Fine Wines

Miravalle 9416
Las Condes – Santiago de Chile
TEL 2 – 220212 | FAX 2 – 2294459

The Frenchman Thierry Villard was amongst the first of the small producers to excite international attention. In 1989 he founded his business together with Santa Emiliana, which aside from the necessary capital put the requisite technology at his disposal. Two wine-growers also contributed their vineyards in the Aconcagua Valley and in Casablanca. Annual production stands at around 300,000 bottles, all of which are exported.

Wine-maker Pablo Morandé's red wines have failed to convince me greatly hitherto. His strength lies in excellent white wines from the cooler sites in both valleys, for which he exclusively uses new barriques, just as much for Chardonnay as for Sauvignon Blanc. The mixture of fruit, lemon freshness and complexity that he achieves with his Chardonnays (***) is achieved by almost no other producer in Chile. His Sauvignon (**) was reminiscent with its clear gooseberry and lychee flavours of the best New Zealand versions of this varietal wine. Unfortunately he now produces a Sauvignon with a less rich bouquet.

Glossary

acidity This is the term for the flavour created by the presence of acids in wine and is described in terms of tartness, freshness and sourness.

acids Description of a group of chemicals. Tartaric, malic and lactic acid amongst others are present in wine and create a fresh, tart flavour. The total acidity of wine is usually expressed in grams of tartaric acid per litre. Normal total acidity for wine is 4-10 grams per litre.

barrique Name of a small oak barrel containing 220-230 litres (58-60.7 gal), which contributes characteristic aromas and flavours when used up to three times. Different types of oak exercise different influences. The Spanish word for such a barrel is *barrica.*

bodega Spanish for wine-cellar. The word is also used to mean a vineyard, winery and wine bar. The proprietor of the bodega is called *el bodeguero.*

bouquet The smell of wine is also often called the nose. Wines with a rich bouquet have a strong smell – which is characteristic of the grape variety as well as the conditions in which the vines grow and are cultivated.

brandy Collective term for all spirits which are made from wine, such as cognac, armagnac, Spanish brandy or Chilean pisco.

cepa Spanish for vine, often used to mean vine variety.

clarification In the fining and stabilization of wine, substances such as bentonite, egg-whites and active carbon amongst others are added to the wine or must so that they combine with unwanted constituents and by a process of precipitation are then removed from the wine. Everyday wines are often clarified several times for the sake of safety or to remedy crass defects.

clarification of must The removal of suspended matter from must to improve the bouquet of the wine.

cosecha Spanish for vintage.

crushing Splitting open of the grape skin and slight crushing of the grapes before pressing.

drip irrigation Irrigation of vineyards by means of a system of irrigation hoses, which are placed in the rows of vines and which dispense an exact amount of water directly over the soil.

dulce Spanish for sweet.

embotellado en origen Spanish for estate bottled.

embotellado por Spanish for bottled by.

fermentation process During the fermentation process the role of winery staff is to supervise the fermentation temperature, the fermentation vessel and the clarity of the must. These three factors influence the bouquet of the wine.

filtration The removal of precipitates from liquids with the help of filters. Various filtration techniques exist for must and wine, which are intended to improve the appearance and bouquet and to avoid any unwanted secondary fermentation or biological activity once the wine has been bottled. Filtration measures to stabilize wine are carried out in particular on everyday wine which is intended for sale in supermarkets. Filtering is avoided as much as is possible in the production of higher quality wines, since it brings about the loss of flavouring agents and nuances of taste at the expense of the wine.

grafting This is a technique in the cultivation of fruit and wine in which two different plants are combined. In the case of wine this became especially important once the phylloxera epidemic had caused such havoc. Wine-growing could continue by grafting phylloxera-susceptible vine varieties on to an immune rootstock. Regrafting is the transfer of an existing vine on to another variety by means of a grafting technique using the old roots.

gran reserva In Chile this is a Spanish term of imprecise meaning for higher quality wine. In Spain it represents the highest level of quality.

maceration To leave the grape must standing together with the grape skins contributes to improving the bouquet of white wine and to increasing the level of tannins in red wine. The Spanish term is *maceración.*

maceración carbonico Spanish term for carbonic maceration, a fermentation method which omits the crushing stage and produces fruity, young red wines in the Beaujolais style.

malolactic fermentation Transformation of malic acid into lactic acid following alcoholic fermentation. The Spanish term is *fermentación malolactica.* This process is virtually always necessary for red wine and makes the wine rounder, mellower and reduces the acid content. When fermenting in new barriques, malolactic fermentation also occurs in many white wines.

must Juice pressed from grapes prior to fermentation.

oxidization Wine defect. The alteration of wine for the worse by its coming into contact with oxygen is recognizable from the smell of slightly rotting apples and often occurs with white wines which are too old, in bottles that have been left open for a time or if errors are made in the cellar. A wine so affected is referred to as being oxidized.

parronales Spanish for pergola system of vine training in vineyards, whereby the vines form a roof about two metres high. The traditional method of cultivation in South America has largely been replaced by the modern *trellis system* today.

phylloxera Insect which destroys the roots of vines. In Europe the phylloxera caused great damage in the nineteenth century and made the grafting of vines necessary. The phylloxera did not spread in South America, and as a result there are still vines which grow on their original rootstocks there.

pressing Extraction of grape must. Heavy pressing increases the volume of juice, but also reduces quality.

raulí barrel Barrel made from South American beechwood which because of the flavour it imparts is used less frequently to store table wines today.

reserva In Chile this is a Spanish term of imprecise meaning for higher quality wine. In Spain the second highest level of quality.

rootstock The roots of a vine on to which the desired vine variety is grafted depending on soil and climate.

seco Spanish for dry. Dry wine has only a small amount of residual sugar, namely sugar which has not turned into alcohol during fermentation.

separation Method of purifying white wine must; precipitates in freshly pressed white wine must can cause fermentation defects and impair the development of the bouquet normally associated with a particular grape variety. If the must is left to stand for several hours at a cooler temperature the heavier precipitates sink to the bottom and can be removed. In larger concerns this process of separation is often carried out by using separators, a method less sparing on the must.

stainless steel tank Stainless steel is the cleanest medium for storing wine which has absolutely no influence on it. Nowadays modern white wines are stored in stainless steel tanks.

tannin Tannin belongs to the chemical group of polyphenolics which are contained in grape skins, pips and stalks as well as in the wood of the barrique. They create a slightly bitter taste in the mouth which also dries it out. Whilst they are desirable in red wines they are jarring in white wines.

trellis system Normal method of vine training in vineyards today using rows secured by wires which are easily managed mechanically.

vendimia Spanish for harvest, grape harvest, also used to mean vintage.

viña Spanish for vineyard, in the sense of an enterprise.

viñedo Spanish for vineyard.

vino Spanish for wine, which in conjunction with the following, means:
~ **blanco** white wine, ~ **corriente** everyday wine, ~ **espumoso** sparkling wine, ~ **fino** fine wine, used generally for quality wine from a stated place of origin, ~ **rosado** rosé wine, ~ **tinto** red wine.

vitis vinifera Subdivision of vines from which nearly all European vine varieties are derived.

yeast Substance consisting of fungous cells which cause sugar to turn into alcohol during fermentation.

Photo Credits

Important Addresses

Chilean Embassy
12 Devonshire Street
London W1N 2DS
Tel. 0171 580 6392 Fax 0171 436 5204

Chilean Consulate General
12 Devonshire Street
London W1N 2DS
Tel. 0171 580 1023 Fax 0171 436 5204

ProChile
c/o Chilean Embassy
12 Devonshire Street
London W1N 2DS
Tel. 0171 580 6392 Fax 0171 255 1848

Wines of Chile (UK) Ltd
Premier House
10 Greycoat Place
London SW1P 1SB
Tel. 0171 222 2073 Fax 0171 222 2083

Wine Export Association
(*Asociación de Exportadores y Embotelladores de Vinos*)
La Pastora 138 Of. C
Las Condes
Santiago de Chile
Tel. 2 234 2503 Fax 2 231 1706

Wine Producers' Association / ChileVid
(*Asociación de Productores de Vinos Finos*)
Hernando de Aguirre 1049 B
Providencia - Santiago
Tel. 56 2 231 9437 Fax 56 2 232 9849

Index